To Marie
"the Cookie Queen"

Congratulations on your job promotion — and many thanks for the fabulous Christmas cookies!

My best,

Jim

HOW AMERICA COOKS TODAY ☆

Woman's Day®
DESSERTS

Sedgewood® Press
New York

The following material was adapted from a previously published book and is used by permission of the publishers:

Strawberry Sorbetto and Honeydew-Melon Sorbetto from *Ice Cream and Ices* by Nancy Arum. Published by Irena Chalmers Cookbooks, Inc.

Photographer Credits

Chris Baker: pages 14, 23, 28, 31, 41, 45, 59
Ben Calvo: pages 8, 25, 37, 50, 52, 56, 69, 74, 81, 84, 102, 117
John Paul Endress: pages 12, 22
Katrina Filary: page 97
Dennis Galante: pages 46, 89, 99, 100, 119, 122
Michael Molkenthin: page 4
Michael Skott: pages 17, 92, 104
Markus Tullis: pages 78-79, 87
Tim Turner: pages 21, 32 (both), 44, 63, 103, 115
John Uher: pages 18, 26, 35, 39, 62, 64, 82, 91, 108, 110, 111, 112, 120, 124

Please address your correspondence to
Customer Service Department,
Sedgewood® Press, Meredith Corporation,
150 East 52nd Street, New York, NY 10022.

For Hachette Magazines, Inc.

Food Editor: Elizabeth Alston
Researchers: Mary Rieger, Marinella Cancio

For Sedgewood® Press

Director: Elizabeth P. Rice
Editorial Project Manager: Maryanne Bannon
Editorial Director: Alison Brown Cerier
Project Editor: Miriam Rubin
Copyeditor: Joan Michel
Designer: Remo Cosentino
Production Manager: Bill Rose

Contents

RECIPE SYMBOLS

At the beginning of many recipes are symbols pointing out which dishes are:

♥ **LOW-CALORIE** (serving under 150 calories)

🕐 **MAKE-AHEAD** (part or all of the recipe can or should be made ahead)

✳ **MICROWAVE** (recipe or variation)

★ **SPECIAL—AND WORTH IT** (in terms of time, calories or expense)

Fruit Desserts

*A fruit dessert can be old-fashioned and comforting,
restaurant-fancy or just sweet and simple.
These wonderful desserts begin with fruits of all kinds
and colors, from all seasons of the year.*

From top: Pear-Ginger Crisp, Apple-Cranberry
Pandowdy, Peach Melba Cobbler

Apples

Apple-Cranberry Pandowdy

The wider the baking dish, the thinner the crust and the faster it bakes and browns. Baking time may also vary with the type of apple used, so test frequently as the end of baking time nears.

FRUIT

- 4 large firm tart apples (about 1¼ pounds) (Granny Smiths are a good choice), peeled, cored and cut in 8 wedges each (about 4 cups)
- 1 cup fresh or frozen cranberries
- ¼ cup packed light-brown sugar
- ½ teaspoon pumpkin-pie spice
- ¼ cup molasses

TOPPING

- 1 cup all-purpose flour
- 2 tablespoons granulated sugar
- 1 teaspoon baking powder
- ⅛ teaspoon salt
- 2 tablespoons cold butter or margarine, cut in small pieces
- ⅓ cup milk
- 1 teaspoon grated fresh orange peel
- ½ cup heavy cream

1. Heat oven to 375°F. Lightly grease a deep 2-quart round baking dish.

2. To prepare fruit: Gently mix apples, cranberries, brown sugar and pumpkin-pie spice in a large bowl until fruit is evenly coated. Stir in molasses. Spoon into prepared dish.

3. Bake 20 to 25 minutes, until apples are not completely cooked but nearly tender when pierced with a fork.

4. Meanwhile, prepare topping: Mix flour, sugar, baking powder and salt in a medium-size bowl. Cut in butter with a pastry blender or two knives until mixture resembles coarse crumbs. Add milk and orange peel and stir gently just until mixture is blended and a soft dough forms.

5. Turn out dough onto a lightly floured surface. With floured fingertips, pat dough into an even circle large enough to cover fruit mixture. Using a floured ¾- to 1½-inch cookie cutter, cut four evenly spaced openings in dough to allow steam to escape from pandowdy; discard cutouts.

6. Remove apple mixture from oven. Carefully place dough over fruit.

7. Bake 40 minutes longer, until topping is golden brown and apples are tender when pierced with a fork.

8. Remove from oven. Pour cream through holes in topping. Serve warm.

Makes 6 servings. Per serving: 332 calories, 3 grams protein, 54 grams carbohydrate, 12 grams fat, 40 milligrams cholesterol with butter, 28 milligrams cholesterol with margarine, 165 milligrams sodium

Golden Apple Crisp

The Golden Delicious apple lends itself well to cooking because it retains its shape and doesn't get mushy.

- 1 container (8 ounces) lemon yogurt
- 1 large egg
- ½ teaspoon ground cinnamon
- 4 large Golden Delicious apples (about 1¾ pounds), peeled, cored and cut in 10 wedges each
- ½ cup all-purpose flour
- ⅓ cup packed brown sugar
- 6 tablespoons cold butter or margarine, cut in small pieces
- ¼ cup chopped walnuts or ¼ cup shredded coconut

1. Heat oven to 350°F. Grease an 8-inch square baking dish.

2. Mix yogurt, egg and cinnamon in a large bowl until well blended. Add apples and toss to coat. Spoon into baking dish.

3. Wipe bowl clean. Add flour and sugar and stir to mix. Cut in butter with a pastry blender or two knives until mixture resembles coarse crumbs.

4. Scatter crumbs evenly over apple mixture. Sprinkle with walnuts.

5. Bake 60 minutes, until apples are tender and top is browned. Remove from oven and let cool a few minutes on a wire rack.

6. Serve warm or at room temperature.

Makes 4 servings. Per serving (with walnuts): 517 calories, 7 grams protein, 70 grams carbohydrate, 25 grams fat, 105 milligrams cholesterol with butter, 51 milligrams cholesterol with margarine, 267 milligrams sodium

Apple Betty

Use tart apples like Greenings, Granny Smiths or crisp Jonathans.

½ cup butter or margarine
3 cups fine crumbs from day-old French or Italian bread (not sourdough) or firm white bread
⅔ cup granulated sugar
¼ teaspoon ground cinnamon
3 large tart apples, peeled, cored and cut in ¼-inch slices (about 4 cups)
Hot Lemon Sauce (recipe follows) or lightly whipped cream

1. Heat oven to 375°F. Grease a 1½-quart soufflé dish or baking dish.

2. Melt butter in a large heavy skillet over medium heat. Add crumbs and cook, stirring constantly, until crisp and deep golden brown. Remove from heat.

3. Mix sugar and cinnamon on a sheet of waxed paper.

4. Sprinkle half the crumbs over the bottom of prepared soufflé dish. Top crumbs with half the apples. Sprinkle with ⅓ cup of the sugar mixture. Add remaining apples. Top with remaining crumbs, then remaining sugar mixture.

5. Bake 35 minutes, until apples are tender when pierced with a fork and topping is well browned.

6. Serve hot or very warm with Hot Lemon Sauce or whipped cream.

Makes 6 generous servings. Per serving (without sauce or cream): 336 calories, 2 grams protein, 47 grams carbohydrate, 16 grams fat, 48 milligrams cholesterol with butter, 0 milligrams cholesterol with margarine, 299 milligrams sodium

Hot Lemon Sauce

½ cup granulated sugar
1 tablespoon cornstarch
⅛ teaspoon salt
1 cup boiling water
1 tablespoon butter or margarine
1½ teaspoons grated fresh lemon peel
3 tablespoons lemon juice
¼ teaspoon ground nutmeg

1. Mix sugar, cornstarch and salt in a small saucepan. Gradually stir in boiling water.

2. Bring to a boil over medium heat, stirring constantly. Boil 1 minute, until sauce is clear and thickened. Remove from heat.

3. Stir butter, lemon peel and juice and nutmeg into sauce. Serve hot over Apple Betty.

Makes 1¼ cups. Per tablespoon: 26 calories, 0 grams protein, 6 grams carbohydrate, 1 gram fat, 2 milligrams cholesterol with butter, 0 milligrams cholesterol with margarine, 21 milligrams sodium

✳ MICROWAVE
Brown-Sugar Baked Apples

This recipe is so fast and simple you'll want to make it often. If you don't have an apple corer, scoop out the cores with a melon baller (but don't scoop through the bottoms of the apples). Rome Beauty is another good choice for baking.

4 medium-size McIntosh apples (about 1¼ pounds)
¼ cup packed brown sugar
2½ tablespoons water
2 teaspoons all-purpose flour
Ground cinnamon to taste
1 tablespoon butter or margarine

1. Core apples, being sure not to cut all the way through. Cut a thin crosswise slice from the top of each.

2. Arrange apples in a microwave-safe glass pie plate. Cover with waxed paper and microwave on high 3 to 4 minutes, rotating dish ¼ turn once.

3. Meanwhile, mix sugar, water, flour and cinnamon in a small bowl until smooth. Spoon evenly over apples and dot with butter.

4. Cover and microwave on high 2 to 3 minutes, until sauce is bubbly and apples are barely tender. Let stand 3 minutes, until tender.

5. Serve, spooning sauce from pie plate over apples.

Makes 4 servings. Per serving: 169 calories, 0 grams protein, 36 grams carbohydrate, 4 grams fat, 9 milligrams cholesterol with butter, 0 milligrams cholesterol with margarine, 41 milligrams sodium

Apple Crunch

¼ cup butter or margarine
½ cup graham-cracker crumbs
½ cup quick-cooking oats
3 tablespoons packed brown sugar
2 tablespoons all-purpose flour
1 teaspoon ground cinnamon
2 pounds Granny Smith apples,
   peeled, cored and thinly sliced
   (about 6 cups)
¼ cup granulated sugar

1. Put butter in a medium-size microwave-safe bowl. Microwave on high about 45 seconds, until butter is melted.

2. Stir in graham-cracker crumbs, oats, brown sugar, flour and cinnamon until blended.

3. Put apples and granulated sugar in an 8-inch square microwave-safe baking dish and toss to mix. Spread evenly in dish. Sprinkle topping evenly over apples.

4. Microwave uncovered on high 8 to 10 minutes, rotating dish ½ turn once, until apples are tender when pierced with a fork. Remove from oven. Let stand directly on a heatproof surface 30 minutes, until topping is firm.

5. Serve warm or at room temperature.

Makes 6 servings. Per serving: 246 calories, 2 grams protein, 42 grams carbohydrate, 9 grams fat, 24 milligrams cholesterol with butter, 0 milligrams cholesterol with margarine, 144 milligrams sodium

Apple Crunch

Baked Apples with Creamy Topping

A good time to make this is when you're using the oven for other baking.

¼ cup chopped walnuts
¼ cup granulated sugar
½ teaspoon ground cinnamon,
   or to taste
6 medium-size apples, cored
   and peeled halfway down from
   stem end
⅓ cup maple-flavor syrup
¼ cup water
Creamy Topping (recipe follows)

1. Heat oven to 425°F. Grease a shallow baking dish large enough to hold apples in a single layer.

2. Mix walnuts, sugar and cinnamon in a small bowl.

3. Place apples in prepared baking dish. Fill centers with nut mixture. Sprinkle any remaining walnut mixture on top. Drizzle with syrup. Pour water into dish.

4. Bake 25 to 30 minutes, until apples are tender but still hold their shape. Remove apples from oven and cool on a wire rack, basting occasionally with pan juices.

5. Cover apples loosely and refrigerate until cold. Serve in dessert bowls and top with the pan juices and a dollop of Creamy Topping.

Makes 6 servings. Per serving (without Creamy Topping): 213 calories, 1 gram protein, 47 grams carbohydrate, 4 grams fat, 0 milligrams cholesterol, 15 milligrams sodium

Creamy Topping

1 cup sour cream
½ cup buttermilk

1. Beat sour cream and buttermilk in a small bowl with a wire whisk or a fork until well blended.

2. Cover and chill until ready to serve. Spoon over baked apples.

Makes 1½ cups. Per tablespoon: 22 calories, 1 gram protein, 1 gram carbohydrate, 2 grams fat, 4 milligrams cholesterol, 3 milligrams sodium

Apples and Cream Dessert

This dessert is like a pie without the crust.

> 5 medium-size apples, peeled, cored
>   and thinly sliced (about 5 cups)
> ¼ cup granulated sugar
> 3 tablespoons all-purpose flour
> 1 cup sour cream
> 1 large egg
> ½ teaspoon vanilla extract
> ¼ cup packed brown sugar
> ¼ teaspoon ground cinnamon

1. Put apples in a 9-inch microwave-safe glass pie plate. Sprinkle with granulated sugar and flour and toss to mix.

2. Cover with a lid or vented plastic wrap. Microwave on high 7 to 9 minutes, stirring once, until apples are tender when pierced with a fork.

3. Meanwhile, mix sour cream, egg and vanilla in a small bowl until blended and smooth.

4. Spread sour-cream mixture evenly over apples. Sprinkle with brown sugar and cinnamon.

5. Cover with waxed paper and microwave on medium-high 4 minutes, rotating dish ¼ turn once, until topping is set around the edges. Let stand uncovered 15 to 20 minutes, until topping is set in the center.

6. Serve warm.

Makes 6 servings. Per serving: 229 calories, 3 grams protein, 35 grams carbohydrate, 9 grams fat, 59 milligrams cholesterol, 35 milligrams sodium

Brown Sugar

☐ Brown sugar is refined, granulated white sugar mixed with molasses to give it a soft, slightly damp texture, brown color and distinctive flavor. Dark-brown sugar has a more intense flavor; light-brown sugar is more delicate. Many of our recipes call for brown sugar without specifying dark or light; that means either can be used, depending on your taste and what's in your pantry.

☐ When a recipe calls for brown sugar, do not substitute granulated or liquid brown sugar; the results may not be the same. To measure brown sugar, always pack it firmly into a dry cup measure. Level off the top with a knife.

☐ To keep brown sugar moist, close the bag or container tightly after using. If the sugar does become hard, add a wedge of apple; seal bag tightly and let stand 1 or 2 days.

Which Apple?

CORTLAND: Resists browning when sliced; a good choice for salads and fruit cups.

GOLDEN DELICIOUS: Holds its shape when cooked and has a tangy-sweet but not tart flavor. A good choice for baking.

GRANNY SMITH: Moderately tart and firm; a good all-around baking and poaching apple.

GREENING: A tart apple good for all baked desserts. Greenings are usually not eaten raw.

IDARED: A firm apple, moderately tart and juicy. Good eaten fresh, baked or poached. Full of flavor.

JONATHAN: An excellent all-purpose apple that holds its shape when baked or poached. Crisp and semi-tart; especially good in mid-September, at the beginning of the apple season.

McINTOSH: Tart and juicy when very fresh, it tends to get mushy with age. Use for sauces.

NEWTON PIPPIN: A very old variety of apple, mildly tart and good eaten fresh and in all desserts.

NORTHERN SPY: Tender, crisp, juicy, this multipurpose apple is good for cooking and baking, best for sauces.

RED DELICIOUS: America's favorite apple is best eaten out-of-hand; not recommended for cooking.

ROME BEAUTY: Very large and bright red; this is a good choice for baked stuffed-apple desserts.

STAYMAN: An apple with a moderately tart flavor; good for all uses.

WINESAP: A firm apple with a tangy, juicy, winelike flavor; perfect for all uses.

Baked Apple-Cranberry Compote

Ginger and lemon give this compote zing. Top with a dollop of sour cream or plain yogurt.

6 medium-size Granny Smith apples
    (about 2 pounds), peeled, cored
    and cut in 8 wedges each
1 can (16 ounces) whole-berry
    cranberry sauce
1 cup water
½ cup raisins
2 tablespoons lemon juice
1 teaspoon ground ginger

1. Heat oven to 425°F.

2. Put all ingredients in a 3-quart casserole and toss gently until well mixed.

3. Bake 40 minutes, until apples are tender but slices are still intact.

4. Serve warm or chilled.

Makes 8 servings. Per serving: 254 calories, 1 gram protein, 66 grams carbohydrate, 1 gram fat, 0 milligrams cholesterol, 5 milligrams sodium

Poached Apples with Brandy Sauce

Can be refrigerated up to one week.

2 cups apple juice
½ teaspoon ground cinnamon
⅛ teaspoon ground nutmeg
Pinch *each* of ground cloves and
    coriander
4 medium-size Red Delicious
    apples, cored, tops and bottoms
    trimmed flat
2 tablespoons brandy or 1 teaspoon
    vanilla extract

1. Bring juice and spices to a boil in a large deep skillet or Dutch oven (not uncoated aluminum) over high heat.

2. Lower apples into liquid, using a spoon. Cover and reduce heat to low. Simmer 20 minutes, until apples are fork-tender. Remove to a serving dish with a slotted spoon.

3. Add brandy to poaching liquid. Raise heat to high and bring to a boil. Reduce heat to medium and simmer uncovered 15 to 20 minutes, until liquid is syrupy and reduced to ¼ cup.

4. Spoon syrup over apples. Serve warm or cover and chill.

Makes 4 servings. Per serving (with brandy): 155 calories, 0 grams protein, 39 grams carbohydrate, 1 gram fat, 0 milligrams cholesterol, 3 milligrams sodium

Successful Whipped Cream

☐ Buy heavy or whipping cream (light cream or half-and-half will not whip successfully). Ultra-pasteurized cream takes slightly longer to whip than fresh heavy cream does.

☐ Cream should always be well chilled before whipping. In hot weather you may wish to chill the bowl and the beaters as well.

☐ Whip cream on high speed with an electric mixer or a rotary beater. If using a portable electric mixer or a rotary beater, choose a deep narrow bowl rather than a wide one so that more of the cream is in contact with the beaters. When beating with a portable mixer or a rotary beater, place the bowl of cream in a sink to catch splashes.

☐ Test cream while whipping by lifting the beaters or dipping into cream with a rubber spatula as it begins to thicken.

☐ Cream used for topping desserts should be softly whipped, only until it is thick and mounds into soft peaks. Serve unsweetened cream over rich, sweet desserts. To sweeten plainer desserts, add confectioners' or granulated sugar before whipping. Or add honey or jam for a mellow flavor. A pinch of ground cinnamon, nutmeg or cardamom adds wonderful flavor; the seeds from a vanilla bean or vanilla extract is a natural.

☐ When cream is to be folded into another mixture, it should be beaten a bit stiffer; the cream is the right consistency when it holds a firm peak that flops over.

☐ Keep a close eye on cream as you whip—a few seconds too long and the cream will turn into butter. If this happens, add a few tablespoons of liquid cream to the whipped cream and beat a few seconds. This will usually work if you haven't gone too far to the butter stage.

☐ Cream may be whipped one to two hours ahead and kept chilled. It will liquefy slightly; rewhip to desired consistency.

Berries

Buttered Berries
(Shown on page 12)

A warm compote. Adjust the amount of sugar in the syrup to the sweetness of the berries and the amount of lemon juice to their tartness. A cross between a hybrid blackberry and a loganberry, the olallieberry is delicious both fresh and cooked and makes excellent jams and jellies.

    1 cup water
    ½ cup granulated sugar, or to taste
    3 cups raspberries, boysenberries,
         blackberries, olallieberries or a
         mixture
    1 teaspoon fresh-squeezed lemon
         juice, or to taste
    1 tablespoon butter or margarine, at
         room temperature
For garnish: extra berries

1. Bring water and sugar to a boil in a medium-size saucepan (not uncoated aluminum) over high heat. Reduce heat to low and simmer about 15 minutes, until slightly syrupy.

2. Add berries to saucepan and simmer 2 minutes, until barely tender (if berries are very soft and ripe, this may mean just heating them through). Drain berries through a strainer suspended over a medium-size bowl. Reserve the syrup.

3. Purée one quarter of the berries with all the reserved syrup in a food processor or a blender. Or, if you wish to remove the seeds, force the berries through a food mill.

4. Immediately return remaining berries, the puréed berries and lemon juice to the saucepan. Heat over medium heat just until warm. Remove from heat and gently swirl in butter until it melts and disappears.

5. Ladle warm berry mixture into dessert bowls. Garnish with extra berries and serve immediately.

Makes 4 servings. Per serving (with raspberries): 174 calories, 1 gram protein, 37 grams carbohydrate, 3 grams fat, 9 milligrams cholesterol with butter, 0 milligrams cholesterol with margarine, 36 milligrams sodium

Jim Dodge's Blueberry-Lemon Cobbler

This talented West Coast pastry chef designed an all-American dessert for *Woman's Day.*

    3 cups fresh blueberries, rinsed and
         drained, or 3 cups frozen
         unsweetened blueberries
    ¾ cup granulated sugar
    2 tablespoons grated fresh lemon peel
    ¾ cup all-purpose flour
    ¼ teaspoon salt
    ¼ teaspoon baking powder
    ⅛ teaspoon baking soda
    3 tablespoons cold butter or
         margarine, cut in small pieces
    1 large egg
    ¼ cup buttermilk
    ¼ teaspoon vanilla extract
Lightly whipped cream

1. Heat oven to 375°F.

2. Toss berries with ½ cup of the sugar and the lemon peel in a 1-quart soufflé dish or other deep baking dish.

3. Mix flour, remaining ¼ cup sugar, the salt, baking powder and baking soda in a medium-size bowl. Cut in butter with a pastry blender or two knives until mixture resembles fine crumbs.

4. Beat egg, buttermilk and vanilla in a small bowl with a fork. Add to flour mixture and stir to mix. Drop spoonfuls of batter over berries.

5. Bake 35 minutes, until topping is a rich golden brown. Remove to a wire rack and let cool slightly.

6. To serve: Spoon warm cobbler into shallow dessert bowls, keeping crust on top. Pass whipped cream at the table.

Makes 5 servings. Per serving (without cream): 322 calories, 4 grams protein, 59 grams carbohydrate, 9 grams fat, 60 milligrams cholesterol with butter, 38 milligrams cholesterol with margarine, 265 milligrams sodium

Blueberry-Orange Cobbler

Whole-wheat flour makes the topping crunchy.

FRUIT

- 2 bags (12 ounces each) frozen unsweetened blueberries (5½ cups)
- 1½ teaspoons grated fresh orange peel
- ½ cup orange juice, preferably fresh-squeezed
- 1 tablespoon cornstarch
- ¼ teaspoon ground nutmeg or mace

TOPPING

- 1 cup all-purpose flour
- ½ cup whole-wheat flour
- 3 tablespoons granulated sugar
- 1 tablespoon baking powder
- ⅛ teaspoon salt
- ⅓ cup cold butter or margarine, cut in small pieces
- ½ cup milk
- 1 teaspoon vanilla extract

1. Heat oven to 400°F.

2. To prepare fruit: Put frozen blueberries in a 9-inch round or 9-inch square baking pan.

3. Mix orange peel and juice, cornstarch and nutmeg in a small bowl. Pour over blueberries and stir to coat.

4. To prepare topping: Mix flours, sugar, baking powder and salt in a medium-size bowl. Cut in butter with a pastry blender or two knives until mixture resembles coarse crumbs. Mix milk and vanilla. Add to flour mixture and stir just until mixture is blended and a dough forms.

5. Turn out dough onto a lightly floured surface. With floured fingertips, pat dough evenly into a 9-inch circle or square. Place over blueberries. Cut slits in dough to allow steam to escape.

6. Bake 40 minutes, until crust is lightly browned and has pulled away from sides of pan and the underside is cooked (check by lifting gently with a spatula; it should be moist but not doughy). Remove from oven to a wire rack to let cool for a few minutes.

7. Serve warm.

Makes 8 servings. Per serving: 249 calories, 4 grams protein, 40 grams carbohydrate, 9 grams fat, 26 milligrams cholesterol with butter, 2 milligrams cholesterol with margarine, 230 milligrams sodium

Clockwise from top: Mango-Lime Sorbet, Plush Peaches and Almond Cookies, Buttered Berries, Honeyed Cantaloupe and Blueberries, Ginger Plums

Grating Citrus Peel

Freshly grated peel adds an intense lively flavor to desserts. The dried peel sold in jars tends to taste bitter. But many cooks find grating peel one of their least favorite tasks. Follow these easy tips so that grating citrus doesn't grate on you.

☐ Grate whole fruits. Grating peel from cut fruit is messy and leads to grated nails and knuckles.

☐ Use a multisided hand grater or one that's specially designed for citrus. Be sure you're using the right surface. A grating surface has sharp holes that look as though a pointed tool has been pushed through, leaving ragged edges to grate the peel. A shredding surface has larger openings with one curved cutting edge and is not good for grating. When the peel will not be cooked, use a fine grating surface. When peel will be cooked, you can use a coarser grating surface.

☐ Press the fruit gently against the grating surface and push downward. Turn fruit slightly and grate from top to bottom again.

☐ Grate only the colored part of the peel, not the bitter white pith underneath.

☐ Work on a sheet of waxed paper to catch the peel. Scrape peel from grater with the point of a small knife. Measure peel loosely packed in measuring spoons. Rinse grater before peel dries. An old toothbrush is good for loosening out all the tiny bits.

☐ After grating the peel, the fruit may then be juiced, if needed for the recipe, saved for another use or eaten.

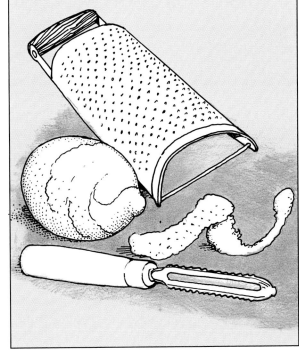

Blueberry-Nectarine Crumble

Serve warm with vanilla ice cream or lightly sweetened whipped cream.

- **8 cups sliced ripe nectarines (6 to 7 large)**
- **1 pint basket blueberries, rinsed and drained (about 3 cups)**
- **1 tablespoon fresh-squeezed lemon juice**
- **1½ cups old-fashioned oats**
- **1 cup packed dark-brown sugar**
- **¾ cup all-purpose flour**
- **1½ teaspoons ground cinnamon**
- **½ teaspoon ground allspice**
- **¾ cup cold butter or margarine, cut in small pieces**

1. Heat oven to 350°F.

2. Mix nectarines, blueberries and lemon juice in a shallow 3-quart baking dish. Spread fruit evenly.

3. Mix oats, sugar, flour and spices in a large bowl. Cut in butter with a pastry blender or two knives until mixture resembles coarse crumbs. Sprinkle over fruit.

4. Bake 50 to 60 minutes, until fruit is fork-tender, juices are bubbly and topping is crisp and lightly browned. Remove from oven to a wire rack to let cool for a few minutes.

5. Serve warm or at room temperature.

Makes 10 servings. Per serving: 369 calories, 4 grams protein, 58 grams carbohydrate, 15 grams fat, 42 milligrams cholesterol with butter, 0 milligrams cholesterol with margarine, 181 milligrams sodium

Blueberry-Nectarine Crumble

Blueberry Shortcakes
(Shown on cover)

Who says shortcakes always have to be filled with strawberries?

- **1 cup all-purpose flour**
- **2 tablespoons granulated sugar**
- **1½ teaspoons baking powder**
- **¼ teaspoon baking soda**
- **¼ teaspoon salt**
- **3 tablespoons solid white vegetable shortening**
- **About ½ cup buttermilk or sour milk (see Note)**
- **Sugared Blueberries (recipe follows)**
- **½ cup heavy cream, whipped to soft peaks (optional)**

1. Heat oven to 450°F. Have an 8-inch layer-cake pan ready.

2. Mix flour, sugar, baking powder, baking soda and salt in a large bowl. Cut in shortening with a pastry blender or two knives until mixture resembles coarse crumbs. Stir in enough buttermilk to make a soft dough.

3. With hands, gently knead dough in bowl ten times. Divide dough into four pieces. Shape each piece into a ball and flatten gently. Arrange dough pieces in cake pan with sides of dough touching.

4. Bake 20 to 25 minutes, until biscuits are lightly browned. Remove from oven. Remove biscuits to a wire rack and let cool just until warm.

5. To assemble shortcakes: Split biscuits and put bottoms on four dessert plates. Spoon one quarter of the Sugared Blueberries on each biscuit bottom. Top with biscuit tops and spoon whipped cream over each, if desired.

6. Serve immediately.

Makes 4 servings. Per serving (with buttermilk, without whipped cream): 369 calories, 5 grams protein, 67 grams carbohydrate, 10 grams fat, 1 milligram cholesterol, 360 milligrams sodium

Note: To make sour milk, add 1½ teaspoons lemon juice or white vinegar to ½ cup milk.

Sugared Blueberries

- **2 cups blueberries**
- **½ cup granulated sugar**
- **1 tablespoon water**

1. Put ½ cup of the blueberries in a medium-size bowl. Mash berries with a pastry blender, a potato masher or a fork.

2. Stir in remaining blueberries, the sugar and water. Let stand at room temperature 1 hour; stir occasionally. Use as directed in Blueberry Shortcakes.

♥ **LOW-CALORIE**

Blueberries with Honey and Lime
(Shown on page 115)

Rub or spray measuring spoons with vegetable oil so that the honey won't stick.

- **1 tablespoon plus 1 teaspoon honey**
- **2 teaspoons fresh-squeezed lime juice**
- **1 pint basket blueberries, rinsed and drained (about 3 cups)**
- **For garnish: lime slices**

1. Mix honey and lime juice in a medium-size serving bowl. Add blueberries. Toss gently to coat.

2. To serve: Spoon into dessert bowls. Garnish with lime slices.

Makes 4 servings. Per serving: 89 calories, 1 gram protein, 22 grams carbohydrate, 1 gram fat, 0 milligrams cholesterol, 1 milligram sodium

---

Blueberries

☐ Choose round berries with no signs of mold. A dusty-looking surface is not mold, merely the bloom on fresh berries. Keep the berries refrigerated until ready to use. Smaller berries have a more intense flavor.

☐ Berry season is short, just the summer months, so freeze fresh blueberries to enjoy year-round. Wash berries just before using, not before freezing. Freeze in a single layer on a baking sheet before transferring to plastic bags or containers. Or if the berries are in a pint box, remove cellophane covering and completely over-wrap container with plastic wrap, covering all air holes. No need to thaw berries before cooking or baking.

Strawberry Fool

A succulent dish you can prepare and chill one to two hours before serving. Adjust sugar to the sweetness of the berries.

1 pint basket strawberries, rinsed and drained (about 3 cups; reserve 4 pretty berries for garnish)
2 tablespoons granulated sugar, or to taste
¾ cup heavy cream

1. Hull and slice all strawberries except those reserved for garnish. Put sliced strawberries in a medium-size bowl and sprinkle with 1 tablespoon of the sugar. Toss gently to mix and coat. Let stand 30 minutes at room temperature, until juices are released.

2. Mash sugared berries with a pastry blender or a potato masher. Strain mashed berries through a strainer, reserving pulp and juice separately.

3. Beat cream with remaining 1 tablespoon sugar until fairly stiff peaks form when beaters are lifted.

4. Fold strawberry pulp into cream just until mixture looks marbleized.

5. Spoon cream mixture into four wine glasses or dessert dishes. Spoon strawberry juice over each. Garnish each with a reserved strawberry and serve.

Makes 4 servings. Per serving: 221 calories, 2 grams protein, 17 grams carbohydrate, 17 grams fat, 59 milligrams cholesterol, 15 milligrams sodium

Strawberries à la Fontainebleau

This American version of the French dessert tastes best at room temperature.

1 package (3 ounces) cream cheese, at room temperature
¼ cup plus ⅓ cup heavy cream
3 tablespoons sour cream
24 whole ripe strawberries with stems or hulls, rinsed and dried
Granulated sugar (optional)

1. Beat cream cheese with an electric mixer on high speed until fluffy. Gradually add ¼ cup of the heavy cream, beating until mixture is soft and smooth.

2. Spoon mixture onto six dessert plates in small flattened mounds.

3. Beat remaining ⅓ cup heavy cream with a wire whisk or an electric mixer (no need to wash bowl or beaters) on high speed until soft peaks form when beaters are lifted.

4. Stir sour cream until smooth. Fold gently into whipped cream. Spoon whipped-cream mixture over cream-cheese mounds. Arrange berries alongside cheese. Sprinkle sugar over each serving, if desired.

Makes 6 servings. Per serving (without sugar): 167 calories, 2 grams protein, 6 grams carbohydrate, 16 grams fat, 49 milligrams cholesterol, 46 milligrams sodium

Strawberries

☐ Once picked, strawberries don't continue to ripen, so it's important to look for shiny berries of a pink to deep-red color with no signs of darkness or wetness and clean crisp-looking caps (hulls). Don't be put off by a white shoulder under the cap—some varieties just grow that way.

☐ Refrigerate strawberries in their baskets, covered, or spread the berries in a single layer and chill. Do not hull or wash until just before serving.

☐ One pint basket equals 3 to 3½ cups whole berries (12 very large to 36 small); about 2¼ cups sliced or 1⅔ cups puréed. One cup whole berries equals about 4 ounces.

Strawberry-Almond Shortcake

🕐 **MAKE-AHEAD**
★ **SPECIAL—AND WORTH IT**

Strawberry-Almond Shortcake

You can bake shortcake layers up to three days ahead. When completely cool, wrap with plastic wrap and store at room temperature. Freeze for longer storage; defrost before assembling cake.

SHORTCAKE LAYERS

- 2 cups all-purpose flour
- 2 teaspoons baking powder
- 1 cup unsalted butter or margarine, at room temperature
- 1 can (8 ounces) almond paste, cut in small pieces (see Note)
- ¼ cup granulated sugar
- ½ cup milk
- 1 large egg
- ½ teaspoon almond extract

FILLING

- 1 quart basket (or 2 pint baskets; about 7 cups) ripe strawberries, rinsed, drained and hulled
- 3 tablespoons granulated sugar
- 1 cup heavy cream
- ½ teaspoon vanilla extract
- For garnish: ¼ cup toasted sliced almonds

1. Heat oven to 375°F. Have ready two un-greased 9-inch round layer-cake pans.

2. To make shortcake: Mix flour and baking powder on waxed paper.

3. Beat butter, almond paste and sugar with an electric mixer on medium-high speed until light and fluffy. Beat in milk, egg and almond extract on medium speed. With mixer on low speed, stir in flour mixture just until blended.

4. Spoon an equal amount of batter into each pan. Spread evenly and smooth tops with a spatula.

5. Bake 20 minutes, until cakes pull away from sides of pans and tops are light golden brown. Let cool in pans on a wire rack 10 minutes. Run a thin metal spatula around inside edges of pans to loosen cakes, then turn out onto racks. Let cool completely.

6. Meanwhile, make filling: Halve enough strawberries to make 2 cups; leave remainder whole.

7. Put halved berries in a small bowl and sprinkle with 2 tablespoons of the sugar. Let stand 30 minutes, tossing occasionally.

8. Beat cream, remaining 1 tablespoon sugar and the vanilla with an electric mixer on high speed until soft peaks form when beaters are lifted.

9. To assemble: Put one shortcake layer on a serving plate top-side up. Top with halved berries and their juices; spread with half the whipped cream. Top with second shortcake layer top-side up. Spread that with remaining whipped cream. Arrange whole berries on top with stem ends down. Sprinkle surface with almonds.

10. Slice cake and serve immediately.

Makes 12 servings. Per serving: 456 calories, 7 grams protein, 40 grams carbohydrate, 32 grams fat, 85 milligrams cholesterol with butter, 37 milligrams cholesterol with margarine, 110 milligrams sodium

Note: If using a 7-ounce roll of soft-type almond paste, add an additional 3 tablespoons all-purpose flour to the cake batter.

Clementines in Caramel Syrup

Thought to be part tangerine, part orange, these fruits have few or no seeds.

6 small clementines or tangerines
1½ cups water
¾ cup granulated sugar

1. Peel clementines, reserving peel from one. Leave fruits whole and remove as much of the stringy white pith as possible. Place clementines in a shallow serving dish and cover.

2. With scissors, cut reserved peel in very thin strips 1 to 2 inches long (there should be about ⅔ cup).

3. Put peel and 1 cup of the water in a small heavy saucepan and bring to a boil over high heat. Reduce heat to medium-low and simmer 5 minutes.

4. Drain off water, reserving the peel.

5. Put ¼ cup of the water and the sugar in saucepan. Stir over medium heat until sugar dissolves. Raise heat to medium-high and bring to a boil. Boil without stirring 6 to 8 minutes, until syrupy and golden around the edges. Shake pan gently to blend colors. When syrup is a light caramel color, remove from heat. (Every second counts; syrup can burn easily and will continue to cook slightly.)

6. Let cool 6 minutes. Add remaining ¼ cup water and the drained peel. (Don't add water sooner or it will spatter. If syrup has cooled too much and starts to harden when water is added, stir over medium heat until syrup liquefies and blends with water.) Let cool 10 minutes.

7. Pierce each clementine in five places with a fork. Pour syrup and peel over fruits; turn to coat. Cover and refrigerate until ready to serve.

Makes 6 servings. Per serving: 129 calories, 1 gram protein, 33 grams carbohydrate, 0 grams fat, 0 milligrams cholesterol, 2 milligrams sodium

Microwave Method: Prepare clementines and peel as directed. Place peel and 1 cup of the water in a 2-cup microwave-safe glass measure. Microwave on high 6 to 7 minutes, until water comes to a boil. Boil 5 minutes; drain. Mix ¼ cup water and the sugar in the measure. Microwave on high 6 to 7 minutes, until mixture begins to turn a light caramel color. Proceed as directed.

Orange-Honey Prunes

Prunes are usually relegated to the breakfast table and are overlooked as the delicious dessert fruit they can be. But it is time for them to come out of the pantry and be treated with respect! Prunes are luscious, rich in flavor and (don't tell the kids) good for you. They blend wonderfully with the orange in this dessert.

1 package (12 ounces) pitted prunes
(2 cups)
½ cup orange juice
¼ cup water
2 tablespoons honey
1 cinnamon stick (3 inches long)
3 whole cloves
1 medium-size orange, peeled, with all
white membrane removed, and cut
in sections
2 slices lemon

1. Put prunes, orange juice and water in a medium-size saucepan. Bring to a boil over high heat. Remove from heat and pour into a medium-size serving bowl.

2. Stir honey, cinnamon stick and cloves into bowl. Add orange and lemon and stir gently.

3. Let cool about 20 minutes and discard cinnamon stick and cloves. Serve warm or cover and refrigerate at least 3 hours or up to 2 weeks.

Makes about 3 cups. Per ½ cup: 189 calories, 2 grams protein, 50 grams carbohydrate, 0 grams fat, 0 milligrams cholesterol, 5 milligrams sodium

Orange-Honey Prunes

Orange and Pineapple Grenadine

Grenadine, a red fruit-flavored syrup, is available in most supermarkets near the cocktail mixes. This dessert also makes a welcome gift at holiday time or anytime.

8 large navel oranges
1 can (20 ounces) pineapple rings in syrup, drained; syrup reserved
1 cup light corn syrup
¼ cup granulated sugar
3 tablespoons slivered crystallized ginger
¼ cup grenadine

1. With a vegetable peeler, remove peel of two of the oranges as thinly as possible. Slice into long ⅛-inch-wide strips (you should have about ½ cup).

2. Peel all of the oranges with a serrated knife, removing all the white membrane. Slice crosswise about the same thickness as the pineapple rings and remove seeds. Set aside.

3. Put strips of orange peel and 1 cup water in a medium-size saucepan. Cover and bring to a boil over high heat. Drain; rinse peel under cold water and drain again. Repeat boiling and draining procedures. Rinse and dry saucepan.

4. Add enough water to reserved pineapple syrup to measure 1 cup. Pour into saucepan. Add corn syrup and sugar. Bring to a boil over high heat, stirring constantly, until sugar dissolves. Reduce heat to medium and simmer 10 minutes.

5. Add boiled orange peel and the ginger to syrup and return to a boil. Cover and simmer over medium heat 30 minutes longer. Remove from heat and stir in grenadine.

6. Arrange fruit in alternating layers in three clean 3-cup glass jars. Pour in hot syrup. Cover tightly and refrigerate up to 10 days.

7. To serve: Spoon fruit and some of the syrup into dessert bowls.

Makes 16 servings. Per serving (with 2 tablespoons syrup): 150 calories, 1 gram protein, 40 grams carbohydrate, 0 grams fat, 0 milligrams cholesterol, 17 milligrams sodium

---

Oranges and Grapefruits

ORANGES: The United States is the world's largest grower of oranges. Since there is such a large crop grown in different areas of the country, the season is virtually year-round, depending on the variety. The greatest supply is available from late fall to early spring. When buying oranges and other citrus fruit, choose those that are heavy for their size and have no soft spots. Minor brown spots or tinges of green on the skin do not affect flavor.

GRAPEFRUITS: The peak season for grapefruit is January through April. Choose fruits that are heavy for their size and have no soft spots. Again, surface blemishes or a few green tinges are nothing to worry about. A pink grapefruit will always have an area of pink blush on the skin.

☐ Keep oranges, grapefruits and other citrus fruit refrigerated for best quality. Picked fully ripe, they will not ripen further at room temperature. Always scrub the peel of citrus fruit well before eating or grating to remove surface chemicals or pesticides.

Fresh Orange-Cranberry Compote
(Shown on page 69)

In the winter, when cranberries are in season, buy extra and freeze several bags for later. Wash just before ready to use.

6 ounces fresh or frozen cranberries (1½ cups)
⅓ cup granulated sugar
¼ cup water
4 juice oranges, peeled with all white membrane removed, sliced in rounds and seeded

1. Put cranberries in a medium-size skillet (not uncoated aluminum). Sprinkle with sugar and add water. Cook over low heat about 3 to 4 minutes, stirring often, until sugar is dissolved and cranberries have popped. Remove from heat.

2. Add orange slices to cranberries. Gently stir and spoon pan juices over the oranges until they are well saturated.

3. Serve warm or chill to serve later.

Makes 6 servings. Per serving: 101 calories, 1 gram protein, 25 grams carbohydrate, 0 grams fat, 0 milligrams cholesterol, 2 milligrams sodium

Winter Fruit Compote

Preserved ginger is available in the Oriental-foods section of your supermarket and in specialty shops.

- **12 ounces whole dried Calimyrna figs, quartered**
- **8 ounces dried apricot halves, cut in half (2 cups)**
- **½ cup orange marmalade**
- **½ cup water**
- **1 tablespoon finely chopped ginger preserved in syrup (optional)**
- **8 ounces fresh or frozen cranberries (2 cups)**
- **3 large grapefruits**
- **6 large navel oranges**
- **4 ounces pitted dates, cut crosswise in thirds (1 cup)**
- **2 medium-size bananas, sliced ¼ inch thick**

1. Stir figs, apricots, marmalade, water and ginger, if desired, in a medium-size saucepan (not uncoated aluminum). Bring to a boil over medium-high heat. Reduce heat to low. Cover and simmer 5 minutes.

2. Stir cranberries into saucepan. Cover and simmer 2 minutes longer. Remove from heat and let cool.

3. Meanwhile, peel grapefruits and oranges with a serrated knife, cutting deep enough to remove white pith. Working over a large serving bowl to collect juices, cut fruit in sections. Squeeze the juice from the membranes. You should have about 3 cups grapefruit and 2 cups orange sections plus combined juice.

4. Add dates, bananas and dried-fruit mixture to grapefruits and oranges and toss gently to mix.

5. Cover and chill at least 2 hours or up to 24 hours before serving.

Makes 12 cups. Per ½ cup: 120 calories, 1 gram protein, 30 grams carbohydrate, 0 grams fat, 0 milligrams cholesterol, 5 milligrams sodium

Wine-Soaked Oranges

A fresh-tasting and sophisticated dessert. Use a good-quality red wine, one that you would serve at the table. You can peel and slice the oranges ahead of time and arrange in the serving dish. Cover and chill until ready to proceed with the recipe.

- **6 navel oranges, 1 scrubbed**
- **2 cups dry red wine**
- **¾ cup granulated sugar**
- **2 teaspoons lemon juice**
- **¼ teaspoon almond or vanilla extract**

1. Remove peel of the scrubbed orange with a vegetable peeler, leaving behind the white membrane. Slice peel in thin strips.

2. Cut white membrane from the peeled orange and then slice the peel and white membrane from the remaining oranges with a serrated knife. Slice oranges in thin rounds and remove seeds. Arrange slices in a large shallow serving dish. Pour wine over oranges and set aside.

3. Put sliced peel in a small saucepan (not uncoated aluminum) and add water to cover. Bring to a boil over high heat and boil 2 minutes. Drain. Repeat procedure and drain well.

4. Mix sugar, ½ cup water and the lemon juice in the saucepan. Stir in drained orange peel. Bring to a simmer over medium-low heat. Reduce heat to low and simmer about 5 minutes, until mixture is syrupy. Remove from heat and stir in almond extract.

5. Pour mixture over oranges and serve.

Makes 6 servings. Per serving: 249 calories, 2 grams protein, 50 grams carbohydrate, 0 grams fat, 0 milligrams cholesterol, 6 milligrams sodium

Melons

♥ LOW-CALORIE
Cantaloupe with Ginger Sugar

For more of a ginger flavor, let prepared melon stand 15 minutes before serving.

> 1 medium-size ripe cantaloupe (2½ to 2¾ pounds), quartered lengthwise and seeded
> 1 tablespoon granulated sugar
> ¼ teaspoon ground ginger

1. Cut between orange flesh and green rind of each melon wedge. Leave flesh on rind in one piece. Cut fruit crosswise in ½-inch-thick slices. Push slices in alternating directions on a serving dish, as shown in photograph.

2. Mix sugar and ginger in a cup. Sprinkle over melon and serve.

Makes 4 servings. Per serving: 97 calories, 2 grams protein, 24 grams carbohydrate, 0 grams fat, 0 milligrams cholesterol, 34 milligrams sodium

Cantaloupe with Raspberry Sauce

Simple and elegant for dessert or at brunch.

> ½ medium-size ripe cantaloupe, seeded and rind cut off
> ½ cup seedless red-raspberry jam
> 1½ teaspoons fresh-squeezed lemon juice
> For garnish: fresh raspberries and mint leaves

1. Put melon cut-side down on a cutting board. Cut melon in half lengthwise, then slice thinly crosswise.

2. Arrange melon on four dessert plates.

3. Stir jam and lemon juice in a small bowl until syrupy. Spoon over melon. Garnish with raspberries and mint leaves and serve.

Makes 4 servings. Per serving: 158 calories, 1 gram protein, 40 grams carbohydrate, 0 grams fat, 0 milligrams cholesterol, 22 milligrams sodium

From left: Cantaloupe with Ginger Sugar, Cantaloupe with Raspberry Sauce

Honeyed Cantaloupe and Blueberries

(Shown on page 12)

If you spray the measuring spoon with no-stick vegetable spray, the honey will slide right off.

- 1½ cups water
- ⅔ cup granulated sugar
- 3 tablespoons mild honey
- 2 teaspoons fresh-squeezed lemon juice
- 1 pint basket blueberries, rinsed and drained
- 3 cups bite-size cubes ripe cantaloupe

For garnish: fresh mint sprigs

1. Bring water and sugar to a boil in a small saucepan over high heat. Reduce heat to low and simmer about 15 minutes, until slightly syrupy. Stir in honey. Remove from heat and stir in lemon juice.

2. Gently mix fruits in a large serving bowl. Pour in syrup and let cool. Cover and chill thoroughly.

3. To serve: Spoon melon, berries and syrup onto dessert plates or into bowls and garnish with mint sprigs.

Makes 6 servings. Per serving: 186 calories, 1 gram protein, 48 grams carbohydrate, 0 grams fat, 0 milligrams cholesterol, 11 milligrams sodium

Cantaloupe and Blueberries with Pernod

This dessert can be refrigerated up to 24 hours, but bring it to room temperature before serving.

- 1 large cantaloupe (about 3½ pounds), halved, seeded and scooped into small balls (about 4 cups)
- 1 pint basket blueberries, rinsed and drained (about 3 cups)
- 2 tablespoons granulated sugar
- 1 tablespoon Pernod or other anise-flavor liqueur such as Ouzo or Sambuca

1. Put melon and berries in a medium-size serving bowl. Sprinkle with sugar; toss to mix and coat. Let stand at room temperature 30 minutes, or until sugar dissolves, stirring two or three times.

2. Stir in Pernod. Serve immediately or cover and chill until ready to serve.

Makes 7 cups. Per cup: 77 calories, 1 gram protein, 19 grams carbohydrate, 0 grams fat, 0 milligrams cholesterol, 12 milligrams sodium

Melon Compote

- ½ medium-size ripe honeydew melon (about 1½ pounds), cut in bite-size chunks
- ½ medium-size ripe cantaloupe (about 1⅓ pounds), cut in bite-size chunks
- ¼ cup thawed frozen orange juice concentrate
- 1 tablespoon light rum or lemon juice
- 6 tablespoons unsweetened flaked coconut

1. Put honeydew, cantaloupe, orange juice and rum in a medium-size bowl. Mix gently; cover and refrigerate about 30 minutes, until chilled.

2. To serve: Spoon into dessert dishes. Sprinkle with coconut.

Makes 6 servings. Per serving (with rum): 121 calories, 2 grams protein, 26 grams carbohydrate, 2 grams fat, 0 milligrams cholesterol, 33 milligrams sodium

Cantaloupe and Blueberries with Pernod

Melon and Grapes with Cinnamon and Cilantro

Melons

☐ To choose a melon, sniff. You can't miss the sweet fragrance of a ripe cantaloupe or honeydew at room temperature. When it yields to gentle pressure, that's another good sign. Also check the stem end; it should have a soft sunken depression and no cut. This means the melon ripened fully on the vine instead of being cut off too soon. The netlike surface on cantaloupes should be raised and evenly distributed. If the melon is not perfectly ripe, leave it at room temperature or in a ripening bowl.

☐ A ripening bowl is a clear acrylic bowl with a perforated domed top. It helps fruit to ripen by trapping the ethylene gas naturally produced by ripening fruit. To speed ripening, add an apple or a ripe banana to the bowl with the less-ripe fruit. Check at least once a day and remove fruit as it becomes ripe, then refrigerate.

☐ Wrap cut melons airtight to keep the aroma from permeating other foods.

🕐 **MAKE-AHEAD**
♥ **LOW-CALORIE**

Melon and Grapes with Cinnamon and Cilantro

Cilantro, also known as fresh coriander or Chinese parsley, is a common ingredient in Mexican and Asian dishes and an unusual dessert flavor that complements these fruits.

  1 **tablespoon fresh-squeezed lime juice**
  1 **tablespoon chopped fresh cilantro**
  ⅛ **teaspoon ground cinnamon**
Pinch of freshly ground pepper
 1½ **cups bite-size chunks cantaloupe**
 1½ **cups bite-size chunks honeydew melon**
  1 **cup halved seedless red grapes**
For garnish: fresh cilantro leaves

1. Mix lime juice, cilantro, cinnamon and pepper in a medium-size serving bowl. Add fruits and toss gently to mix and coat.

2. Serve at once or cover and chill until ready to serve.

3. Just before serving, garnish with cilantro leaves.

Makes 4 servings. Per serving: 67 calories, 1 gram protein, 17 grams carbohydrate, 0 grams fat, 0 milligrams cholesterol, 16 milligrams sodium

🕐 **MAKE-AHEAD**
♥ **LOW-CALORIE**

Watermelon with Raspberry Sauce

Perfect for hot summer nights. If you wish, sprinkle with a few fresh raspberries or blackberries just before serving.

  1 **package (10 ounces) frozen raspberries in syrup, thawed**
  6 **cups bite-size chunks watermelon, seeded, if desired (from 4- to 5-pound melon)**

1. Process raspberries with syrup in a food processor or a blender until almost puréed but still chunky.

2. Put watermelon in a large serving bowl. Pour in puréed raspberries and toss gently to coat. Cover and refrigerate at least 30 minutes, or until well chilled, before serving.

Makes 6 servings. Per serving: 100 calories, 1 gram protein, 24 grams carbohydrate, 1 gram fat, 0 milligrams cholesterol, 4 milligrams sodium

Peaches

Peach-Strawberry Cobbler

You can also bake this cobbler in a cast-iron pan. Top servings with slightly softened vanilla ice cream or frozen yogurt. Pass ground ginger in a shaker to sprinkle over the cobbler.

1¾ **pounds ripe peaches, peeled (see Peaches, at right), halved, pitted and sliced (about 4 cups)**
  2 **cups sliced fresh strawberries**
  1 **tablespoon fresh-squeezed lemon juice**
  1 **cup all-purpose flour**
  1 **cup granulated sugar**
  ½ **teaspoon salt**
  1 **large egg, lightly beaten**
  6 **tablespoons cold butter or margarine, cut in small pieces**

1. Heat oven to 375°F.

2. Gently toss peaches and strawberries with lemon juice in an 11x6-inch or 8-inch square or other shallow baking pan. Spread fruit in an even layer.

3. Mix flour, sugar and salt in a medium-size bowl. Add egg and toss with a fork until the mixture is crumbly. Sprinkle flour mixture evenly over fruit. Dot with butter.

4. Bake about 45 minutes, until the filling is bubbly. If the top is not a rich golden brown, place under broiler for a few seconds. Remove from oven to a wire rack to let cool for a few minutes.

5. Serve warm with your choice of toppings.

Makes 6 servings. Per serving (without topping): 387 calories, 4 grams protein, 66 grams carbohydrate, 13 grams fat, 68 milligrams cholesterol with butter, 32 milligrams cholesterol with margarine, 331 milligrams sodium

Peaches

☐ A pretty red blush on a peach is not a sign of ripeness. Look for a yellowish or creamy background, smooth unblemished skin and fruit that yields to gentle pressure. Aroma is important, too. At room temperature a ripe peach has that wonderfully unique peachy smell. If peaches are not fully ripened, do not refrigerate. Keep in a ripening bowl (see Melons, page 23) or in a loosely closed paper bag until ready to use or eat. Then refrigerate. Peaches are most abundant during June, July and August.

☐ Peeling peaches takes a bit of trouble, but in some recipes it is essential. Bring a medium-size saucepan of water to a boil over high heat. Dip peaches one at a time in boiling water with a slotted spoon 30 seconds to 1 minute, depending on ripeness of peaches. Remove from saucepan with slotted spoon. Cool peaches quickly under cold running water or in a bowl of cold water. Slip off skins and proceed with the recipe. Unripe or out-of-season peaches may be next to impossible to peel, and there is really no remedy for this. It's best to make fresh peach desserts when peaches are at their peak.

☐ One pound of fresh peaches will equal 2 large or 3 medium-size peaches, 2 cups peeled and sliced, 1⅔ cups peeled and diced or 1½ cups peeled and puréed peaches.

Peach Melba Cobbler

(Shown on page 4)

The combination of peaches and raspberries is a classic.

FRUIT

- 1 **bag (20 ounces) frozen sliced peaches (about 4 cups)**
- 1⅓ **cups frozen unsweetened raspberries (about 6 ounces)**
- ¼ **cup granulated sugar**
- 2 **teaspoons cornstarch**

BISCUIT DOUGH

- 1 **cup all-purpose flour**
- ¼ **cup granulated sugar**
- 1½ **teaspoons baking powder**
- ⅛ **teaspoon salt**
- ⅛ **teaspoon ground nutmeg**
- ¼ **cup cold butter or margarine, cut in small pieces**
- ½ **cup sour cream**

1. Heat oven to 375°F. Generously grease a shallow 1½-quart baking dish.

2. To prepare fruit: Toss peaches and raspberries with sugar and cornstarch in a large bowl until evenly coated. Spoon into prepared dish.

3. Bake fruit 20 minutes, until hot and juicy.

4. Meanwhile, prepare biscuit dough: Mix flour, sugar, baking powder, salt and nutmeg in a medium-size bowl. Cut in butter with a pastry blender or two knives until mixture resembles coarse crumbs. Add sour cream and stir gently with a wooden spoon just until a sticky dough forms.

5. Drop dough in 6 large spoonfuls onto the hot fruit mixture.

6. Return to the oven and bake 30 to 35 minutes longer, until biscuits are golden brown. Remove from oven to a wire rack to let cool for a few minutes.

7. Serve warm.

Makes 6 servings. Per serving: 268 calories, 4 grams protein, 38 grams carbohydrate, 12 grams fat, 32 milligrams cholesterol with butter, 8 milligrams cholesterol with margarine, 229 milligrams sodium

🕐 **MAKE-AHEAD**
Easy Peach Crisp for Two

Mix up one or more batches of the granola mixture ahead of time; keep covered in the refrigerator for up to a week to make this whenever you like.

- 1 **tablespoon butter or margarine**
- ½ **cup unsweetened granola**
- ¼ **cup packed dark-brown sugar**
- ½ **teaspoon ground cinnamon**
- 1 **can (16 to 17 ounces) sliced yellow cling peaches in juice, drained**

1. Heat oven to 375°F. Have ready two 6- to 8-ounce ramekins or other small ovenproof dishes ready.

2. Melt butter in a small saucepan over low heat. Add granola, brown sugar and cinnamon and mix well. Remove from heat.

3. Arrange peaches in ramekins. Sprinkle half the granola mixture over each.

4. Bake 15 minutes, until hot and browned.

5. Let cool a few minutes before serving.

Makes 2 generous servings. Per serving: 374 calories, 3 grams protein, 72 grams carbohydrate, 10 grams fat, 18 milligrams cholesterol with butter, 0 milligrams cholesterol with margarine, 138 milligrams sodium

Easy Peach Crisp for Two

Fresh Peach Crumble

✳ MICROWAVE
Fresh Peach Crumble

This luscious crumble bakes in the microwave in about 10 minutes, but it needs 30 minutes of standing time before serving so that temperatures can equalize and the topping firm up.

2½ pounds ripe peaches, peeled (see
  Peaches, page 24), halved, pitted
  and sliced (about 6 cups)
 ½ teaspoon grated fresh lemon peel
 1 tablespoon lemon juice
 6 tablespoons cold butter or
  margarine, cut in small pieces
 ⅔ cup all-purpose flour
 ⅔ cup quick-cooking oats
 ¼ cup packed dark-brown sugar
 ¼ cup granulated sugar
 1 teaspoon ground cinnamon
 ½ teaspoon ground allspice
 ½ cup coarsely chopped walnuts or pecans

1. Put peaches in a shallow 9-inch round microwave-safe baking dish. Sprinkle with lemon peel and juice.

2. Put flour in a medium-size bowl. Cut butter into flour with a pastry blender or two knives until mixture resembles coarse crumbs. Stir in oats, brown and granulated sugars, cinnamon, allspice and the walnuts.

3. Sprinkle crumb mixture evenly over peaches and press crumbs down lightly.

4. Microwave uncovered on high 8 to 10 minutes, rotating dish ½ turn once, until peaches are tender when pierced with a fork.

5. Let stand directly on a heatproof surface 30 minutes, until warm and topping is firm.

6. Sprinkle with walnuts and serve warm.

Makes 6 to 8 servings. Per serving (one sixth; with walnuts): 383 calories, 5 grams protein, 52 grams carbohydrate, 19 grams fat, 36 milligrams cholesterol with butter, 0 milligrams cholesterol with margarine, 145 milligrams sodium

Conventional Method: Heat oven to 375°F. Have ready a 9-inch round layer-cake pan. Assemble as directed. Bake 45 to 50 minutes, until peaches are tender when pierced with a fork.

🕐 **MAKE-AHEAD**

★ **SPECIAL—AND WORTH IT**

Plush Peaches

(Shown on page 12)

Crisp cookies are topped with brandied peaches, vanilla ice cream and whipped cream—a truly elegant dessert. Store any leftover cookies in an airtight container.

ALMOND COOKIES

Whites from 2 large eggs
2 teaspoons beaten whole egg
⅔ cup granulated sugar
1 tablespoon butter or margarine, melted
½ teaspoon almond extract
⅛ teaspoon vanilla extract
⅓ cup all-purpose flour

PEACHES

4 cups thinly sliced fresh peaches
1 tablespoon fresh-squeezed
    lemon juice
⅓ cup granulated sugar
4 teaspoons brandy (optional)
1 pint premium-quality vanilla
    ice cream
1 cup heavy cream, lightly whipped
    with 2 tablespoons granulated
    sugar and ¾ teaspoon vanilla extract
3 tablespoons lightly toasted sliced
    almonds

1. To make cookies: Heat oven to 400°F. Generously butter (must be butter) several cookie sheets.

2. Beat egg whites, beaten egg and sugar in a large bowl with a fork or a wire whisk just until blended. Beat in butter and extracts. Stir in flour.

3. Drop 6 level measuring-teaspoonfuls of dough on a prepared cookie sheet, leaving plenty of space between each. Spread each mound into a 2-inch circle with the back of a spoon.

4. Bake cookies 4 minutes, until a rich golden color. Immediately remove cookies with a flexible metal spatula to a wire rack to let cool. (If cookies are hard to remove, return to the oven briefly to warm.) Repeat with remaining batter, making sure that cookie sheets are cool and well buttered before each use.

5. To prepare peaches: Gently mix peaches, lemon juice, sugar and brandy, if desired, in a medium-size bowl. Let stand 30 minutes to draw out juices. If desired, cover and chill.

6. To serve: Place one cookie in the bottom of each of six dessert glasses, top with a scoop of ice cream, then peaches, whipped cream and a sprinkling of almonds. Serve with another cookie tucked into each. Pass remaining cookies at the table.

Makes 6 servings. Per serving (without cookies): 313 calories, 4 grams protein, 28 grams carbohydrate, 22 grams fat, 71 milligrams cholesterol, 42 milligrams sodium

Makes 36 cookies. Per cookie: 23 calories, 0 grams protein, 5 grams carbohydrate, 0 grams fat, 3 milligrams cholesterol with butter, 2 milligrams cholesterol with margarine, 7 milligrams sodium

Stuffed Peaches

Have these ready to go before you put dinner on the table. Bake peaches just before serving them; it takes only a few minutes.

6 canned peach halves, well drained
½ cup blanched slivered almonds
⅓ cup packed brown sugar
¼ cup raisins
1 tablespoon chopped candied
    orange peel
1 teaspoon chopped crystallized ginger
Pinch of salt
¼ cup honey
2 tablespoons light or dark rum

1. Heat oven to 350°F.

2. Arrange peaches cut-side up in a 9-inch square baking dish.

3. Mix almonds, brown sugar, raisins, orange peel, ginger and salt in a small bowl. Spoon into peach cavities.

4. Mix honey and rum in a cup or glass measuring cup and drizzle over peaches.

5. Bake about 12 minutes, until peaches are heated through and bubbly.

6. Serve hot or warm.

Makes 6 servings. Per serving: 152 calories, 2 grams protein, 27 grams carbohydrate, 5 grams fat, 0 milligrams cholesterol, 29 milligrams sodium

---

Honey

The lighter the color of the honey, the milder its taste. When the label lists no flower source, the honey comes from several kinds of flowers.

Honey-Bourbon Peaches

① **MAKE-AHEAD**
♥ **LOW-CALORIE**
✳ **MICROWAVE**

Honey-Bourbon Peaches

You'll need fragrant unblemished peaches that feel slightly soft when gently pressed.

> 6 **cups water**
> 1½ **cups granulated sugar**
> ½ **cup honey**
> ¼ **cup fresh-squeezed lemon juice**
> 1 **large lemon, scrubbed and sliced in thin rounds**
> 2 **cinnamon sticks (each 2 to 3 inches long)**
> 4 **whole cloves**
> 8 **medium-size ripe peaches (about 2½ pounds)**
> 3 **tablespoons bourbon or sour-mash whiskey**

1. Put water, sugar, honey, lemon juice, lemon slices, cinnamon sticks and cloves in a Dutch oven (not uncoated aluminum). Bring to a boil over high heat, stirring until sugar and honey dissolve. Reduce heat to medium-low; simmer 5 minutes.

2. Add peaches and reduce heat until syrup ripples but doesn't quite simmer. Cover and poach 10 minutes, turning peaches occasionally, until tender when pierced with a fork. Remove from syrup to a plate with a slotted spoon.

3. When peaches are cool enough to handle, slip off skins. Halve and pit peaches. Put halves in a large serving bowl. Add poached lemon slices.

4. Strain 1½ cups of the syrup through a strainer suspended over a 2-cup glass measure or a small bowl. Stir in the bourbon and pour syrup over peaches.

5. Cover and chill until ready to serve.

Makes 8 servings. Per serving (with 3 tablespoons syrup): 113 calories, 1 gram protein, 30 grams carbohydrate, 0 grams fat, 0 milligrams cholesterol, 2 milligrams sodium

Microwave Method: Mix poaching-liquid ingredients as directed in a 4-quart microwave-safe bowl. Cover with a lid or vented plastic wrap and microwave on high 15 to 18 minutes, until boiling. Boil 4 minutes. Add peaches; cover and microwave on high 3 to 4 minutes, until almost tender when pierced with a fork. Let stand covered 5 minutes, until tender. Proceed as directed.

Vanilla-Poached Peaches with Raisins

Save the leftover poaching liquid and refrigerate to use again.

6 cups water
1¾ cups granulated sugar
2 tablespoons fresh-squeezed
   lemon juice
6 medium-to-large ripe peaches
   (about 2 pounds)
¼ cup golden raisins
1 tablespoon vanilla extract
2 teaspoons orange- or peach-flavor
   liqueur (optional)

1. Put water, sugar and lemon juice in a large deep saucepan or Dutch oven (not uncoated aluminum). Bring to a boil over high heat, stirring until sugar dissolves. Reduce heat to medium-low. Cover and simmer 5 minutes.

2. Add peaches and reduce heat until syrup ripples but doesn't quite simmer. Cover and poach peaches 15 to 20 minutes, turning occasionally, until tender when pierced with a fork.

3. Remove peaches from syrup to a plate with slotted spoon. Cover syrup to keep warm. As soon as peaches are cool enough to handle, slip off skins.

4. Put peeled peaches in a large serving bowl. Pour 4 cups hot syrup into a 4-cup glass measure. Stir in raisins, vanilla and liqueur, if desired. Pour over peaches.

5. Cover and chill until ready to serve.

Makes 6 servings. Per serving (with liqueur): 204 calories, 1 gram protein, 53 grams carbohydrate, 0 grams fat, 0 milligrams cholesterol, 3 milligrams sodium

Microwave Method: Mix water, sugar and lemon juice in a 3- to 4-quart microwave-safe bowl or casserole. Cover with a lid or vented plastic wrap and microwave on high 15 to 18 minutes, until boiling. Boil 3 to 4 minutes to let flavor develop. Add peaches. Cover and microwave on high 3 to 4 minutes, until peaches are almost tender when pierced with a fork. Let stand covered 5 minutes, until tender. Proceed as directed.

Caramel Peaches

½ cup granulated sugar
1 cup boiling water
2 teaspoons fresh-squeezed
   lemon juice
5 medium-size ripe peaches, sliced

1. Put sugar in a medium-size heavy skillet over medium heat. Stir sugar until it has melted completely, begins to smoke and turns a rich amber brown. Immediately remove skillet from heat. Stand back (mixture will sputter) and, stirring constantly, pour in the boiling water.

2. Return the sugar mixture to medium heat and simmer, stirring constantly, until caramelized sugar dissolves and syrup is smooth. Remove from heat; stir in lemon juice.

3. Place peaches in a deep heatproof serving bowl. Pour the hot syrup over peaches. Cool, turning fruit occasionally. Cover and chill. Serve cold.

Makes 6 servings: Per serving: 153 calories, 1 gram protein, 40 grams carbohydrate, 0 grams fat, 0 milligrams cholesterol, 8 milligrams sodium

Peaches and Plums with Vanilla-Rum Syrup

Make with one or more variety of plums.

2 cups water
1 cup granulated sugar
1 vanilla bean (see Vanilla, page 61)
3 tablespoons gold (medium) rum
1 tablespoon fresh-squeezed
   lemon juice
8 small ripe red and/or purple plums
   (about 1 pound), halved and pitted
5 small ripe peaches (about 1½
   pounds), peeled (see Peaches, page
   24), halved and pitted

1. Stir water and sugar in a medium-size saucepan. Cut vanilla bean in half lengthwise; scrape out seeds with tip of a small knife. Add the seeds and bean to saucepan. Bring to a boil over high heat, stirring to dissolve sugar. Reduce heat to low; simmer 20 minutes. Remove from heat. Remove vanilla bean. Stir in rum and lemon juice.

2. Put plums and peaches in a deep serving bowl. Pour in the hot syrup. Cool, turning fruit occasionally. Cover and chill at least 8 hours before serving.

Makes 6 servings. Per serving: 216 calories, 1 gram protein, 53 grams carbohydrate, 0 grams fat, 0 milligrams cholesterol, 3 milligrams sodium

Peaches Brûlée

Plums or nectarines can be substituted for the peaches.

4 small-to-medium-size peaches (about 1 pound), halved and pitted
¾ cup sour cream
1 tablespoon granulated sugar
¼ teaspoon grated fresh orange peel
¼ teaspoon vanilla extract
⅛ teaspoon ground nutmeg
¼ cup packed light-brown sugar

1. Turn on broiler. Place peach halves cut-side up in a single layer in a shallow baking dish.

2. Mix sour cream, granulated sugar, orange peel, vanilla and nutmeg in a small bowl. Spoon mixture over peaches. Sprinkle with brown sugar.

3. Broil about 6 inches from heat source 4 to 5 minutes, until brown sugar melts and peaches are hot but barely cooked.

4. Serve peaches immediately or cover and chill until ready to serve.

Makes 4 servings. Per serving: 193 calories, 2 grams protein, 28 grams carbohydrate, 9 grams fat, 19 milligrams cholesterol, 28 milligrams sodium

⏱ **MAKE-AHEAD**
♥ **LOW-CALORIE**
✳ **MICROWAVE**

Honey-Baked Peaches

For best results, use fragrant ripe peaches.

4 medium-size ripe peaches (about 1¼ pounds), peeled (see Peaches, page 24), halved and pitted
¼ cup honey
¼ cup water
2 tablespoons packed light-brown sugar
1 tablespoon lemon juice
2 strips lemon peel (each about 2 inches long), removed with a vegetable peeler

1. Arrange peaches cut-side up in an 8-inch square microwave-safe baking dish.

2. Mix honey, water, brown sugar and lemon juice in a small bowl until blended. Pour over peaches. Add lemon peel.

3. Cover with a lid or vented plastic wrap and microwave on high 5 to 6 minutes, turning peaches over once, until almost tender when pierced with a fork. Let stand covered 5 minutes, until tender. Discard lemon peel.

4. Serve warm or refrigerate until ready to serve.

Makes 4 servings. Per serving: 124 calories, 1 gram protein, 33 grams carbohydrate, 0 grams fat, 0 milligrams cholesterol, 2 milligrams sodium

Honey-Lime Peaches

Sweet honey and tangy lime over peaches and ice cream.

¾ cup mild honey
1½ teaspoons grated fresh lime peel
3 tablespoons fresh-squeezed lime juice
1 pint premium-quality vanilla ice cream
6 medium-size ripe peaches, peeled (see Peaches, page 24), halved and thinly sliced

1. Mix honey and lime peel and juice in a small bowl.

2. Put a shallow scoop of ice cream in each of six dessert bowls or wide-bowled stemmed glasses. Top ice cream with peaches. Drizzle with honey-lime mixture. Serve immediately.

Makes 6 servings. Per serving: 258 calories, 3 grams protein, 56 grams carbohydrate, 5 grams fat, 18 milligrams cholesterol, 30 milligrams sodium

🕐 MAKE-AHEAD
♥ LOW-CALORIE

Gingered Peach and Plum Compote

Ripe fruit assures a juicy compote.

3 tablespoons granulated sugar
2 tablespoons chopped crystallized
    ginger
1 tablespoon fresh-squeezed
    lemon juice
1 pound ripe peaches (about 3 medium-
    size), peeled (see Peaches, page
    24), halved, pitted and cut in thin
    wedges
3 cups sliced very ripe plums
1 cup halved ripe fresh strawberries
    (large berries quartered)

1. Mix sugar, ginger and lemon juice in a large serving bowl. Add fruits and toss gently to mix and coat.

2. Cover and refrigerate 1 hour to blend flavors before serving.

Makes 8 servings. Per serving: 69 calories, 0 grams protein, 18 grams carbohydrate, 0 grams fat, 0 milligrams cholesterol, 3 milligrams sodium

♥ LOW-CALORIE
Java Peaches

Try this delicious combination of coffee and peaches. It could easily become a favorite, and it's made in minutes.

3 large ripe peaches, cut in thin wedges
1 pint frozen coffee yogurt or coffee ice
    cream
3 teaspoons freeze-dried instant coffee
    granules, or to taste

1. Arrange peach wedges in a pinwheel design on 6 dessert plates.

2. Place a scoop of frozen yogurt in the center of each pinwheel and sprinkle with the instant coffee.

3. Serve immediately.

Makes 6 servings. Per serving (with frozen yogurt): 104 calories, 3 grams protein, 22 grams carbohydrate, 1 gram fat, 3 milligrams cholesterol, 0 milligrams sodium

Peach-Blueberry Compote with Toasted Almonds

🕐 MAKE-AHEAD
♥ LOW-CALORIE
Peach-Blueberry Compote with Toasted Almonds

Orange marmalade sweetens this compote.

½ cup slivered almonds
¼ cup orange juice, preferably
    fresh-squeezed
3 tablespoons orange marmalade
2 teaspoons orange-flavor liqueur
    (optional)
1 pound ripe peaches (about 3
    medium-size), peeled (see Peaches,
    page 24), halved, pitted and sliced
    in thin wedges
2 cups fresh blueberries, rinsed and
    drained

1. Shake almonds in a small skillet over medium heat until toasted. (Or toast in your microwave oven; see Microwave Tips for Desserts, page 33.) Transfer to a plate to let cool.

2. Mix juice, marmalade and liqueur, if desired, in a medium-size serving bowl. Add peaches and blueberries to juice mixture. Toss gently to mix and coat.

3. Serve immediately or cover and chill. Sprinkle with almonds just before serving.

Makes 6 servings. Per serving (with liqueur): 122 calories, 2 grams protein, 18 grams carbohydrate, 5 grams fat, 0 milligrams cholesterol, 3 milligrams sodium

Peaches with Peach Sauce

Peaches and Cream

Peaches with Peach Sauce

For fewer calories, use all-fruit sugar-free peach spread instead of preserves.

⅔ **cup peach preserves**
4 **teaspoons fresh-squeezed**
   lemon juice
2 **teaspoons orange- or peach-flavor**
   liqueur (optional)
2 **teaspoons water**
4 **medium-size ripe peaches (about**
   1½ pounds)
For garnish: fresh mint leaves

1. Mix preserves, lemon juice, liqueur, if desired, and water in a small bowl until blended. Spoon onto four dessert plates.

2. Cut each peach in half and remove pit (no need to peel). Cut halves in thin crosswise slices. To arrange: Put one peach half on each plate, leaving slices together. Arrange slices of second peach half like a fan around the first, as shown in photograph.

3. Garnish with mint leaves and serve immediately.

Makes 4 servings. Per serving (with liqueur): 209 calories, 1 gram protein, 54 grams carbohydrate, 0 grams fat, 0 milligrams cholesterol, 8 milligrams sodium

♥ **LOW-CALORIE**
Peaches and Cream

Sounds rich and tastes luscious, but weighs in at less than 150 calories per serving.

4 **medium-size ripe peaches (about**
   1¼ pounds)
1 **tablespoon granulated sugar**
1 **teaspoon orange- or peach-flavor**
   liqueur (optional)
⅓ **cup heavy cream**
For garnish: fresh mint leaves

1. Put enough water to cover two of the peaches in a medium-size saucepan. Bring water to a boil over high heat. Add two peaches and cook 1 to 2 minutes. Remove to a bowl of cold water to let cool. Slip off skins or pull off with a small knife. Halve and pit peaches, then cut in small chunks.
2. Put peach chunks in a food processor or a blender. Add sugar and liqueur, if desired, and process until smooth. Pour into a small bowl and stir in cream.

3. Halve and pit remaining two peaches (no need to peel).

4. To serve: Spoon sauce into four dessert bowls. Add a peach half cut-side up to each bowl. Garnish with mint leaves.

Makes 4 servings. Per serving (with liqueur): 143 calories, 2 grams protein, 19 grams carbohydrate, 9 grams fat, 35 milligrams cholesterol, 9 milligrams sodium

---

Microwave Tips for Desserts

WARM CITRUS FRUIT: Oranges and lemons yield more juice when warmed slightly before squeezing. Microwave on high 20 seconds or until warm to the touch.

MELT JELLY OR JAM: Spoon into a microwave-safe bowl or cup measure. Microwave until melted, stirring every 30 seconds (½ cup takes 60 to 90 seconds on high).

SOFTEN HARD BROWN SUGAR: Place in a microwave-safe bowl. Sprinkle lightly with water and close package or cover loosely. Microwave on high, checking every 15 to 30 seconds, until softened (15 seconds for amounts less than ½ pound).

SOFTEN BUTTER OR MARGARINE: For easy creaming or spreading, microwave on medium until softened (½ cup takes 10 to 30 seconds). If butter begins to melt, remove from oven and let stand until the desired consistency.

TOAST COCONUT: Spread shredded or flaked coconut in a thin layer on a glass pie plate. Microwave on high just until coconut starts to brown lightly in spots (30 seconds to 3 minutes depending on amount of coconut). Continue to microwave, stirring every 30 seconds, until evenly toasted, keeping in mind that coconut will continue to brown after you remove it from the oven.

TOAST NUTS: Place in a microwave-safe pie plate. Microwave on high until very lightly browned, stirring once during cooking (1 cup chopped nuts takes 4 to 6 minutes).

WARM EGG WHITES: Egg whites whip to a greater volume when at room temperature. Place in a microwave-safe bowl. Microwave on high to remove the chill (2 whites take about 15 seconds).

Pears

Pear-Ginger Crisp

(Shown on page 4)

To crush gingersnaps, use a food processor or a blender or place in a heavy plastic bag and crush with a rolling pin.

FRUIT

- 1 can (29 ounces) pear halves packed in heavy syrup, drained (reserve ¼ cup syrup)
- 1 tablespoon all-purpose flour
- 1 tablespoon lemon juice
- 1 tablespoon honey
- ½ teaspoon ground ginger

TOPPING

- 14 gingersnaps, finely crushed (¾ cup)
- 2 tablespoons packed light-brown sugar
- 2 tablespoons cold butter or margarine, cut in small pieces
- ¼ cup sliced almonds

1. Heat oven to 375°F.

2. To prepare fruit: Arrange pear halves cut-side down in a 9-inch pie plate.

3. Mix reserved pear syrup, the flour, lemon juice, honey and ginger in a small bowl until well blended. Pour evenly over pears.

4. To prepare topping: Mix cookie crumbs and brown sugar in a medium-size bowl. Cut in butter with a pastry blender or two knives until mixture resembles coarse crumbs. Sprinkle crumbs around pears. Sprinkle almonds on top.

5. Bake 20 minutes, until juices bubble. Remove from oven to a wire rack to let cool for a few minutes.

6. Serve warm.

Makes 4 servings. Per serving: 350 calories, 3 grams protein, 67 grams carbohydrate, 11 grams fat, 28 milligrams cholesterol with butter, 10 milligrams cholesterol with margarine, 223 milligrams sodium

○ **MAKE-AHEAD**
✳ **MICROWAVE**

Poached Pears with Raspberries

Can be prepared up to two days ahead.

- 2 cans (12 ounces each) apricot nectar (3 cups)
- ¼ cup apricot jam or preserves
- 2 teaspoons ground ginger
- 8 small firm ripe pears (about 3 pounds)
- 1 cup fresh or frozen unsweetened raspberries (from a 12-ounce bag)

For garnish: fresh mint leaves (optional)

1. Choose a saucepan or a deep skillet (not uncoated aluminum) wide enough to hold halved pears in a single layer, slightly overlapping if necessary.

2. Stir nectar, jam and ginger in saucepan until blended. Bring to a boil over medium-low heat. Reduce heat to low; cover and simmer about 5 minutes to blend flavors.

3. Meanwhile, peel pears. Halve lengthwise, leaving stem on one half of each pear if possible. Scoop out cores with a melon baller or a small spoon.

4. Gently add pears to simmering liquid with a large spoon. Simmer uncovered 10 minutes, gently turning pears twice, until tender when pierced in thickest part with a fork.

5. Cool pears in saucepan. Transfer pears and poaching liquid to a medium-size bowl. Cover tightly and refrigerate until chilled.

6. To serve: Spoon two pear halves and about ¼ cup poaching liquid into each of eight dessert bowls. Add a few raspberries to each. Let stand 30 minutes at room temperature. Garnish with mint leaves, if desired.

Makes 8 servings. Per serving: 195 calories, 2 grams protein, 49 grams carbohydrate, 1 gram fat, 0 milligrams cholesterol, 5 milligrams sodium

Microwave Method: Mix nectar, jam and ginger in a deep 3-quart microwave-safe casserole. Cover with a lid or vented plastic wrap. Microwave on high 6 to 8 minutes, until boiling. Boil 2 to 3 minutes to blend flavors. Peel, halve and core pears as directed. Add to liquid. Cover and microwave on high 5 to 6 minutes, until almost tender when pierced in thickest part with a fork. Let stand covered 6 minutes, until tender. Proceed as directed.

Marmalade-Poached Pears

2 medium-size firm ripe pears, peeled,
    halved and cored
1 cup pineapple juice
2 tablespoons orange marmalade
2 tablespoons golden raisins

1. Put pears cut-side down in a single layer in a large saucepan or Dutch oven (not uncoated aluminum).

2. Add juice, marmalade and raisins to pears. Bring to a boil over medium-high heat. Reduce heat to low. Cover and simmer 12 to 15 minutes, until pears are fork-tender.

3. Serve warm, at room temperature or chilled, with poaching liquid and raisins spooned over top.

Makes 4 servings. Per serving: 121 calories, 1 gram protein, 31 grams carbohydrate, 0 grams fat, 0 milligrams cholesterol, 3 milligrams sodium

Choosing Pears

☐ Pears are a very delicate fruit and bruise easily, which is why they're picked and shipped while green and hard. Pears are in peak supply from September through November but are available year-round.

☐ When perfectly ripe, pears are really a treat, requiring nothing but a napkin to wipe the juice from your arms. However, you can cook with not-so-ripe pears with good results.

☐ Pears are ripe when they yield slightly to gentle pressure and are fragrant at room temperature. Ripen them at home in a ripening bowl (see Melons, page 23) or at room temperature in a loosely closed paper bag. Refrigerate when ripe.

☐ Peel pears with a stainless-steel swivel-blade vegetable peeler or a small sharp knife. Carbon-steel blades or peelers will discolor the pears. You can peel and core pears to be used for poaching up to an hour ahead. To prevent browning, submerge them in a bowl of warm water mixed with a tablespoon of lemon juice.

Marmalade-Poached Pears

Poached Pears with Currant Jelly

Strain the leftover poaching syrup into a glass jar and refrigerate to use again. Or add fruit juices and ginger ale to make a sparkling fruit punch.

- 2 cups water
- 1 cup granulated sugar
- 2 tablespoons lemon juice
- 6 medium-size firm ripe pears
- ¼ cup currant jelly

For garnish: fresh mint leaves (optional)

1. Put water, sugar and 1 tablespoon of the lemon juice in a large saucepan or Dutch oven (not uncoated aluminum). Bring to a boil over high heat, stirring to dissolve sugar. Reduce heat to low. Cover and simmer 5 minutes.

2. Meanwhile, peel pears, leaving stems intact. Cut a small slice off the bottoms of pears so that they stand upright. Brush with remaining 1 tablespoon lemon juice.

3. Add pears to syrup. Cover pears and simmer about 20 minutes, turning occasionally, until tender when pierced at the bottom with a fork.

4. Carefully remove pears with a slotted spoon to a high-sided serving platter large enough to hold them standing upright.

5. Melt jelly in a small saucepan over low heat. Spoon over pears.

6. Chill thoroughly. Just before serving, garnish with mint leaves, if desired.

Makes 6 servings. Per serving: 200 calories, 1 gram protein, 51 grams carbohydrate, 1 gram fat, 0 milligrams cholesterol, 6 milligrams sodium

Glazed Brandied Pears

(Shown on page 112)

If pears don't stand upright, cut a thin sliver from the bottoms.

- ½ cup packed light-brown sugar
- ⅓ cup brandy
- 1 tablespoon butter or margarine
- 2 teaspoons cornstarch
- ½ teaspoon vanilla extract
- ¼ teaspoon ground nutmeg
- ⅛ teaspoon ground cloves
- 4 medium-size ripe Anjou, Bartlett or Comice pears, peeled and cored
- 4 cinnamon sticks (each 3 inches long)

1. Stir sugar, brandy, butter, cornstarch, vanilla, nutmeg and cloves in a 2-cup glass measure. Microwave uncovered on high 2 to 3 minutes, stirring once, until thick and clear.

2. Meanwhile, stand pears upright in a 9-inch microwave-safe pie plate and put a cinnamon stick in the center of each, where the stem was. Pour the hot sauce in and around pears.

3. Cover with a lid or vented plastic wrap and microwave on high 4 to 5 minutes, rotating dish ¼ turn and rearranging pears once.

4. Microwave on medium 2 to 3 minutes longer, until pears are almost tender. Let stand covered 10 minutes, until tender.

5. Serve warm.

Makes 4 servings. Per serving: 248 calories, 1 gram protein, 49 grams carbohydrate, 3 grams fat, 9 milligrams cholesterol with butter, 0 milligrams cholesterol with margarine, 46 milligrams sodium

Pears with Strawberry Sauce

⏱ **MAKE-AHEAD**
♥ **LOW-CALORIE**

Pears with Strawberry Sauce

Any fine restaurant would be proud of this elegant presentation. The sauce—which can be made up to eight hours ahead—goes well with all kinds of berries and with vanilla or fruit-flavored ice cream and sherbet.

2 **cups sliced fresh strawberries**
2 **tablespoons granulated sugar**
1 **teaspoon lemon juice**
2 **large ripe pears**
To garnish: fresh mint leaves

1. Put strawberries, sugar and lemon juice in a blender or a food processor and process until smooth. Cover and chill until ready to use.

2. Peel pears and cut in half lengthwise, leaving stems attached to two of the halves. Remove cores with a melon baller or a small spoon. Make a V-shaped cut at bottom of each pear half to remove blossom end.

3. Place pears cut-side down on a cutting board. Starting one third down from stem end, cut each half in very thin lengthwise slices with a sharp knife.

4. Pour one fourth of the strawberry sauce on each of four dessert plates. Gently press pear halves with palm of hand to fan out slices. Remove pears to plates with a spatula or a pancake turner.

5. Garnish stem ends with mint leaves and serve immediately, or chill for a few minutes but no longer or pears will darken.

Makes 4 servings. Per serving: 104 calories, 1 gram protein, 25 grams carbohydrate, 1 gram fat, 0 milligrams cholesterol, 3 milligrams sodium

Pineapples

Pineapple-Banana Crisp

Tropical fruits in an old-fashioned crisp.

FRUIT

3 medium-size bananas, sliced
    ½ inch thick (about 2 cups)
1 can (20 ounces) pineapple chunks
    in juice, drained (reserve
    ¼ cup juice)
2 tablespoons apricot preserves

TOPPING

½ cup old-fashioned or quick oats
½ cup packed light-brown sugar
¼ cup all-purpose flour
¼ cup flaked coconut
¼ cup cold butter or margarine, cut in
    small pieces

1. Heat oven to 400°F.

2. To prepare fruit: Gently mix bananas and pineapple in a shallow 1½-quart baking dish. Stir preserves into reserved pineapple juice and pour over fruit mixture.

3. To prepare topping: Mix oats, sugar, flour and coconut in a medium-size bowl. Cut in butter with a pastry blender or two knives until mixture resembles very coarse crumbs. Sprinkle evenly over fruit mixture.

4. Bake 15 to 20 minutes, until topping is lightly browned and juices are bubbly. Remove from oven to a wire rack to let cool for a few minutes.

5. Serve warm.

Makes 6 servings. Per serving: 361 calories, 3 grams protein, 64 grams carbohydrate, 12 grams fat, 24 milligrams cholesterol with butter, 0 milligrams cholesterol with margarine, 101 milligrams sodium

⏱ MAKE-AHEAD
Pineapple Brown-Sugar Crisp

1 large ripe pineapple (about
    4 pounds), peeled, quartered,
    cored and cut in 1-inch chunks
    (about 6 cups)
¼ cup granulated sugar
1 tablespoon quick-cooking tapioca
1 cup all-purpose flour
1 cup packed light-brown sugar
½ cup cold unsalted butter or
    margarine, cut in small pieces

1. Heat oven to 375°F.

2. Put pineapple in a deep 2-quart baking dish. Sprinkle with granulated sugar and tapioca and toss to mix.

3. Mix flour and brown sugar in a medium-size bowl until blended. Cut butter in with a pastry blender or two knives until mixture is crumbly. Sprinkle over pineapple.

4. Bake 40 minutes, until juices are bubbly and top is brown and crisp.

5. Remove from oven and let cool on a wire rack. Serve warm or let cool completely.

Makes 8 servings. Per serving: 349 calories, 2 grams protein, 61 grams carbohydrate, 12 grams fat, 31 milligrams cholesterol with butter, 0 milligrams cholesterol with margarine, 11 milligrams sodium

---

Pineapples

☐ Look for a green leafy crown. Press pineapple gently; it should yield slightly to gentle pressure, but the bottom should not be very soft or leaking juice (signs of overripe or rotting fruit). The pineapple should have a clean, sweet (not musty) fragrance. Refrigerate ripe pineapples and use as soon as possible; they tend to ferment if kept too long.

☐ To peel pineapple, cut off top and bottom; stand pineapple upright. Cut off skin in strips with a sharp knife until completely peeled, cutting deep enough to remove the eyes. Quarter pineapple lengthwise; remove core and cut fruit in chunks.

☐ Many markets sell pineapples already peeled and cored. You can also buy pineapple chunks from the supermarket. An automatic corer that removes core, rind and crown is a handy kitchen gadget.

Stuffed Pineapple with Macadamia-Rum Dressing

Stuffed Pineapple with Macadamia-Rum Dressing

A refreshing finale for a picnic or a barbecue.

MACADAMIA-RUM DRESSING

¾ cup sour half-and-half
     (light sour cream)
⅓ cup pineapple juice
2 tablespoons rum or 1½ teaspoons
     rum flavoring
2 teaspoons packed brown sugar
⅓ cup coarsely chopped
     macadamia nuts

FRUIT

1 large ripe pineapple (about 5 pounds)
1 large ripe papaya, peeled, seeded and
     cut in thin slices (about 2 cups)
1 firm ripe mango (about 14 ounces),
     halved, pitted, peeled and cut in
     ½-inch chunks
1 cup bite-size pieces watermelon
1 cup bite-size pieces honeydew melon
1 cup green or red seedless grapes
½ pint basket strawberries, rinsed,
     drained, hulled and sliced (about
     1¼ cups)

2 ripe apricots, halved, pitted and cut
     in thin wedges
1 ripe kiwifruit, peeled and thinly
     sliced
1 ripe star fruit (carambola), thinly
     sliced (optional)

1. To prepare dressing: Put all dressing ingredients in a medium-size bowl and stir until blended. Cover and refrigerate until ready to use.

2. To prepare fruit: Cut pineapple in half lengthwise from bottom through the leafy crown. Remove core by cutting out a lengthwise V-shaped wedge. Cut fruit from each half with a serrated curved grapefruit knife or a small sharp paring knife, leaving ¼-inch-thick shells.

3. Put shells in freezer for ½ hour, until partially frozen. (This helps support the fruit salad and keeps it chilled longer.)

4. Cut pineapple fruit in bite-size pieces and put in a large bowl.

5. Add remaining fruits to pineapple and mix gently.

6. To serve: Spoon fruit into pineapple shells. Pour sauce into a pitcher or bowl and pass at the table.

Makes 10 cups, 10 servings. Per serving (with 2 tablespoons dressing): 209 calories, 2 grams protein, 38 grams carbohydrate, 6 grams fat, 7 milligrams cholesterol, 14 milligrams sodium

♥ LOW-CALORIE

Fruit-Filled Pineapple with Ginger Sauce

Kiwi and papaya are ripe when they are fragrant and feel soft but not squishy when gently pressed.

One 3½- to 4-pound fresh ripe
    pineapple
 1 large ripe papaya (about 1 pound),
    halved lengthwise, seeds scooped
    out, peeled and cut in bite-size
    chunks
 1 ripe kiwifruit, peeled, halved and
    thinly sliced
 1 cup pineapple juice
 ½ cup granulated sugar
 1 tablespoon finely chopped
    crystallized ginger

1. Cut pineapple in half lengthwise from bottom through the leafy crown. Remove core by cutting out a lengthwise V-shaped wedge. Cut fruit from each half with a serrated curved grapefruit knife or a small sharp paring knife, leaving ½-inch-thick shells. Wrap and refrigerate shells. Cut pineapple fruit in bite-size pieces; place in a large nonmetal bowl. Add papaya and kiwi.

2. Mix pineapple juice, sugar and ginger in a small saucepan (not uncoated aluminum). Bring to a boil over high heat. Reduce heat to medium-low and simmer 5 minutes. Remove from heat and let cool to room temperature.

3. Pour syrup over fruits and toss to coat. Cover and chill several hours or overnight.

4. To serve: Transfer fruits to reserved pineapple shells with a slotted spoon. Pour juice left in bowl into a pitcher and serve with fruit.

Makes 6 servings. Per serving: 147 calories, 1 gram protein, 38 grams carbohydrate, 0 grams fat, 0 milligrams cholesterol, 3 milligrams sodium

♥ LOW-CALORIE

Pineapple-Berry Bowl

Best made not more than one hour ahead.

 1 tablespoon granulated sugar
 ½ teaspoon grated fresh lime peel
 2 teaspoons fresh-squeezed lime juice
 1 small ripe pineapple (about 2½
    pounds), peeled, cored and cut in
    small chunks (see Pineapples,
    page 38)
 1 large ripe kiwifruit, peeled and sliced
 1 pint basket strawberries, rinsed,
    drained, hulled and halved
 1 tablespoon sesame seed, toasted
    (see Note)

1. Mix sugar, lime peel and juice in a large serving bowl. Add pineapple and kiwifruit and toss to mix and coat.

2. Let fruit stand at room temperature at least 15 minutes, stirring two to three times, until sugar dissolves. Gently stir in strawberries.

3. Before serving, sprinkle with sesame seed.

Makes 6 servings. Per serving: 101 calories, 1 gram protein, 24 grams carbohydrate, 1 gram fat, 0 milligrams cholesterol, 3 milligrams sodium

Note: Shake sesame seed in a small skillet over medium heat until seeds are lightly toasted and begin to pop.

✳ MICROWAVE

Glazed Pineapple

1½ cups packed light-brown sugar
 ½ cup maple or maple-flavored syrup
 1 tablespoon vanilla extract
 1 teaspoon ground cinnamon
 ¼ teaspoon ground nutmeg
 1 ripe pineapple (about 3 pounds),
    peeled, cored and cut in 1-inch
    spears (see Pineapples, page 38)

1. Mix all ingredients except the pineapple in a deep 2-quart microwave-safe casserole.

2. Microwave uncovered on high 2 to 3 minutes, stirring once, until sugar has dissolved.

3. Add pineapple and turn to coat. Microwave on high 6 to 8 minutes, stirring sauce and turning pineapple twice, until sauce is slightly thickened and pineapple very tender. Let stand 5 minutes.

4. Spoon onto dessert plates and serve warm.

Makes 8 servings. Per serving: 254 calories, 0 grams protein, 64 grams carbohydrate, 0 grams fat, 0 milligrams cholesterol, 15 milligrams sodium

Plums

★ SPECIAL—AND WORTH IT

Plum Shortcake

A thin crust of biscuit dough topped with rows of summer plums that release their juices when baked. This cake is best served the day it's made or reheated in a low oven before serving.

FRUIT

1½ **pounds very ripe plums (about 6 medium-size), cut in thin wedges (about 4½ cups)**
1 **tablespoon fresh-squeezed lemon juice**

CRUST

1½ **cups all-purpose flour**
½ **cup plus 1 tablespoon granulated sugar**
1 **teaspoon baking powder**
Pinch of salt
5 **tablespoons cold butter or margarine, cut in small pieces**
¼ **cup milk**
1 **large egg**
1 **teaspoon vanilla extract**
Nutmeg Cream (recipe follows)

1. Heat oven to 375°F. Have ready a baking sheet and a 13x9-inch metal baking pan.

2. To prepare fruit: Toss plums with lemon juice in a large bowl.

3. To prepare crust: Mix flour, ½ cup of the sugar, baking powder and salt in a large bowl. Cut in butter with a pastry blender or two knives until mixture resembles fine crumbs.

4. In 1-cup glass measure (used to measure the milk) or in a small bowl, beat milk, egg and vanilla with a fork until well blended. Pour over flour mixture and mix with a fork. (Dough will be soft and sticky.)

5. Scrape dough into baking pan and spread evenly. (Don't overwork dough or it will toughen.) Arrange plums overlapping on dough in four long rows, leaving a ¼-inch border around the edges. Sprinkle plums with remaining 1 tablespoon sugar.

6. Place pan on baking sheet. Bake 30 minutes, until edges are browned and have shrunk from sides of pan. Remove shortcake from baking sheet and let cool in pan on a wire rack.

7. Serve warm or cool with Nutmeg Cream.

Makes 12 servings. Per serving (without Nutmeg Cream): 149 calories, 2 grams protein, 22 grams carbohydrate, 6 grams fat, 32 milligrams cholesterol with butter, 15 milligrams cholesterol with margarine, 103 milligrams sodium

Nutmeg Cream

1½ **cups heavy cream**
1 **tablespoon granulated sugar**
¼ **teaspoon freshly grated or ground nutmeg**

1. Beat cream and sugar with an electric mixer on high speed until soft peaks form when beaters are lifted. Stir in nutmeg. Serve with Plum Shortcake.

Makes 3 cups. Per ¼ cup: 109 calories, 1 gram protein, 2 grams carbohydrate, 11 grams fat, 40 milligrams cholesterol, 10 milligrams sodium

Plum Shortcake

Plum Cobbler

Serve plain or with half-and-half, lightly whipped cream or a small scoop of vanilla ice cream or ice milk.

FRUIT

1½ **pounds assorted ripe plums, halved, pitted and cut in ½-inch wedges (about 4½ cups)**
¼ **cup packed light-brown sugar**
1 **tablespoon dark Jamaican rum or 1 teaspoon vanilla extract**

DOUGH

1⅔ **cups all-purpose flour**
2 **tablespoons granulated sugar**
1½ **teaspoons baking powder**
⅛ **teaspoon salt**
5 **tablespoons cold butter or margarine, cut in small pieces**
¾ **cup milk**

1. Heat oven to 425°F.

2. To prepare fruit: Put plums in a shallow 1½-quart baking dish. Add brown sugar and rum and toss until evenly coated. Bake 15 to 20 minutes, stirring twice, until fruit is hot and juicy.

3. Meanwhile, prepare dough: Mix flour, sugar, baking powder and salt in a medium-size bowl. Cut in butter with a pastry blender or two knives until mixture resembles coarse crumbs. Add milk and stir gently with a wooden spoon just until a sticky dough forms.

4. Drop dough by large spoonfuls onto hot fruit mixture.

5. Return to oven and bake 20 to 35 minutes longer, until dumplings are golden brown. Remove from oven to a wire rack.

6. Serve warm or at room temperature.

Makes 6 servings. Per serving (with rum): 338 calories, 5 grams protein, 54 grams carbohydrate, 11 grams fat, 34 milligrams cholesterol with butter, 4 milligrams cholesterol with margarine, 261 milligrams sodium

Plum Betty

Serve warm topped with a dollop of sour cream, or pass a pitcher of heavy cream at the table.

2 **pounds prune-plums, halved and pitted (about 4 cups)**
½ **cup packed light-brown sugar**
½ **cup old-fashioned oats**
½ **cup chopped walnuts**
3 **tablespoons all-purpose flour**
5 **tablespoons cold butter or margarine, cut in small pieces**

1. Heat oven to 400°F. Grease a 9-inch square baking dish.

2. Arrange plums in prepared baking dish.

3. Mix sugar, oats, walnuts and flour in a medium-size bowl. Work butter in with fingers until mixture is crumbly. Sprinkle over plums.

4. Bake 30 minutes, until juices are bubbly and topping is golden brown. Remove from oven to a wire rack to let cool for a few minutes.

5. Serve warm or at room temperature.

Makes 8 servings. Per serving: 256 calories, 3 grams protein, 36 grams carbohydrate, 13 grams fat, 23 milligrams cholesterol with butter, 0 milligrams cholesterol with margarine, 93 milligrams sodium

---

Plums

☐ Plums come in numerous varieties in a rainbow of colors, from light yellow-green to deep purple-black. The California plum season begins in mid-May and runs through September.

☐ Plums are ripe and ready to eat when they yield to gentle palm pressure and are slightly soft at the tip end. Unripe plums may be ripened at home in a ripening bowl (see Melons, page 23) or at room temperature in a loosely closed paper bag.

☐ Pit plums by cutting through the fruit along the seam, then twisting neatly in half. Cut or pull away the pit from one side. When a plum does not pit easily, simply slice the fruit off the pit in wedges.

Ginger Plums
(Shown on page 12)

¾ cup water
½ cup granulated sugar
¼ cup chopped crystallized ginger
1 teaspoon fresh-squeezed
    lemon juice
1¾ pounds plums, halved, pitted and
    cut in thin wedges (about 4 cups)
1 pint vanilla ice cream
For garnish: 1 tablespoon finely grated
    unsweetened chocolate

1. Bring water, sugar and ginger to a boil in a small saucepan over high heat. Reduce heat to low and simmer 10 minutes, until slightly syrupy. Remove from heat and add lemon juice.

2. Put plums in a medium-size bowl. Pour in syrup and mix. Let cool, tossing plums occasionally. Cover and chill thoroughly.

3. To serve: Scoop ice cream into six dessert bowls, top with plums and syrup and sprinkle with chocolate.

Makes 6 servings. Per serving: 245 calories, 3 grams protein, 51 grams carbohydrate, 5 grams fat, 18 milligrams cholesterol, 33 milligrams sodium

Plum and Nectarine Sundaes

Summer's bounty in a bowl, enhanced by the brightness of lime sherbet and the crunch of macadamia nuts.

7 ripe plums, cut in ½-inch wedges
3 medium-size ripe nectarines, cut in
    bite-size chunks
2 cups ripe strawberries, hulled (cut
    larger berries in half)
2 tablespoons fresh-squeezed
    lime juice
1 quart lime sherbet
¼ cup coarsely chopped macadamia
    nuts or almonds

1. Mix plums, nectarines, strawberries and lime juice in a large bowl. Cover and chill at least 30 minutes, until well chilled.

2. To serve: Scoop sherbet into 6 dessert dishes. Top each with some of the fruit mixture. Sprinkle with nuts and serve immediately.

Makes 6 servings. Per serving: 351 calories, 4 grams protein, 63 grams carbohydrate, 12 grams fat, 9 milligrams cholesterol, 61 milligrams sodium

Poached Plums in Almond Syrup

The short prune-plum season is at its peak in September; this recipe is a wonderful way to enjoy that special fruit. Tip: When toasting nuts for a dessert, make more than you need, cool and store in the freezer. That way you'll have extra around to add crunch to a dish of plain ice cream or sliced fruit.

2 cups water
¾ cup granulated sugar
1½ pounds prune-plums, halved and
    pitted (about 3 cups)
¼ cup almond-flavor liqueur (see
    Note)
¼ teaspoon almond extract
For garnish: 2 tablespoons toasted
    slivered almonds

1. Stir water and sugar in a large saucepan (not uncoated aluminum). Bring to a boil over medium heat. Add plums and reduce heat to low. Cover and simmer 10 to 15 minutes, until plums are just tender when pierced with a fork but still retain their shape.

2. Transfer plums to a medium-size bowl with a slotted spoon.

3. Return syrup to a boil over medium-high heat. Reduce heat to low and simmer about 15 minutes, until syrup is thickened and reduced by half. Remove from heat.

4. Stir almond liqueur and extract into syrup. Pour over plums. Let cool, then chill at least 1 hour before serving.

5. To serve: Spoon plums and syrup into dessert bowls and sprinkle with almonds.

Makes 6 servings. Per serving (with liqueur): 209 calories, 2 grams protein, 44 grams carbohydrate, 3 grams fat, 0 milligrams cholesterol, 2 milligrams sodium

Note: You can omit the liqueur and increase almond extract to ½ teaspoon.

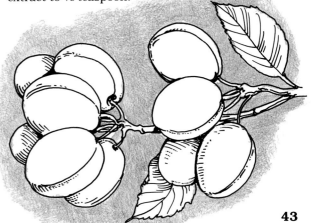

Plums with Brown Sugar

You can use just one kind of plum, but this dessert is even more delicious when you mix two or more varieties.

2 pounds assorted ripe plums, halved, pitted and cut in ½-inch wedges
2 tablespoons packed light-brown sugar

1. Put plums and sugar in a medium-size bowl and toss gently to mix and coat. Let stand 30 minutes at room temperature to blend flavors.

2. Spoon into dessert bowls and serve.

Makes 6 servings, 1 cup each. Per serving: 86 calories, 1 gram protein, 22 grams carbohydrate, 0 grams fat, 0 milligrams cholesterol, 3 milligrams sodium

Plums with Rum and Sour Cream

The rum brings out the flavor of the plums.

2 pounds assorted ripe plums, halved, pitted and cut in ½-inch wedges
2 tablespoons packed light-brown sugar
2 tablespoons dark Jamaican rum or ½ teaspoon vanilla extract
1 cup sour cream

1. Put plums, sugar and rum in a medium-size bowl. Toss gently to mix and coat. Let stand 30 minutes to blend flavors.

2. Spoon into six serving bowls. Top with sour cream and serve.

Makes 6 servings, 1 cup plums each. Per serving (with rum): 179 calories, 2 grams protein, 24 grams carbohydrate, 8 grams fat, 17 milligrams cholesterol, 23 milligrams sodium

Plums with Brown Sugar

Mixed Fruits

⏱ MAKE-AHEAD
Fruits in Berry Sauce

You can use a combination of any available fruits. The sauce can be made a day ahead.

BERRY SAUCE

1 cup fresh strawberries, rinsed, drained, hulled and halved
1 package (10 ounces) frozen red raspberries in syrup, thawed
¼ cup confectioners' sugar
1 tablespoon lemon juice
⅛ teaspoon ground cinnamon (optional)

FRUITS

1 cup fresh strawberries, rinsed, drained, hulls left on
2 medium-size ripe bananas, halved lengthwise and crosswise
1 cup seedless green grapes

1. To make berry sauce: Process strawberries and raspberries in a food processor or a blender until smooth. Strain through a fine strainer suspended over a medium-size bowl. Discard seeds.

2. Add confectioners' sugar, lemon juice and cinnamon, if desired, to puréed berries and stir until blended. Cover and refrigerate until ready to serve.

3. To serve: Spoon about ½ cup of the sauce into each of four deep dessert bowls. Arrange fruits over sauce and serve immediately.

Makes 4 servings. Per serving: 203 calories, 2 grams protein, 51 grams carbohydrate, 1 gram fat, 0 milligrams cholesterol, 3 milligrams sodium

Mint Julep Compote

⏱ MAKE-AHEAD
♥ LOW-CALORIE
Mint Julep Compote

A perfect dessert for a Derby Day party.

1 cup water
⅓ cup granulated sugar
¼ cup chopped fresh mint leaves
¼ cup bourbon (optional)
3 cups fresh pineapple chunks
2 cups cantaloupe balls
1 cup seedless red or green grapes or pitted sweet cherries
2 nectarines (about 8 ounces), cut in bite-size pieces
1 large pear (about 8 ounces), peeled, cored and cut in bite-size pieces
For garnish: additional chopped fresh mint

1. Stir water, sugar and mint in a small saucepan. Bring to a boil over high heat and boil 3 minutes. Remove from heat. Strain through a fine strainer into a large serving bowl and let stand until cool. Stir in bourbon, if desired.

2. Add fruit to syrup in bowl and toss gently to mix. Cover and chill thoroughly, about 1 to 2 hours.

3. To serve: Mix gently and garnish with additional mint.

Makes 8 servings. Per serving (with bourbon): 139 calories, 1 gram protein, 31 grams carbohydrate, 0 grams fat, 0 milligrams cholesterol, 8 milligrams sodium

Puddings, Mousses and Soufflés

Creamy puddings, dreamy custards, feather-light mousses and elegant soufflés—each of these recipes makes a dessert to remember.

(Clockwise from left) Brandy-Alexander Mousse, Baked Custard with Jelly Syrup and Coach House Bread Pudding with Raspberry Sauce

Chocolate Puddings

🕐 MAKE-AHEAD
Creamy Chocolate Pudding

Everyone's favorite.

1 package (3⅝ ounces) chocolate
    pudding and pie-filling mix (not
    instant pudding)
2 tablespoons unsweetened cocoa
    powder (preferably Dutch-
    process cocoa)
2 cups milk
1 cup heavy cream
2 tablespoons granulated sugar

1. Stir pudding mix, cocoa and milk in a medium-size heavy saucepan. Cook according to package directions until thickened and smooth. Remove from heat and let cool, stirring occasionally.

2. Beat cream and sugar with an electric mixer at high speed until stiff peaks form when beaters are lifted. Fold half of the cream into pudding until well blended.

3. Spoon pudding into six goblets or a medium-size serving bowl. Garnish with remaining whipped cream.

4. Cover and chill at least 1 hour before serving.

Makes 6 servings. Per serving: 210 calories, 3 grams protein, 21 grams carbohydrate, 14 grams fat, 48 milligrams cholesterol, 103 milligrams sodium

🕐 MAKE-AHEAD
Chocolate Pots de Crème

Silky chocolate pudding with a French accent.

4 squares (1 ounce each) semisweet
    chocolate, melted (see Melting
    Chocolate, at right)
1 recipe freshly prepared Basic Stirred
    Custard (recipe on page 60)
½ cup heavy cream (optional)

1. Stir chocolate into custard until well blended.

2. Spoon into eight 5-ounce pots de crème cups, demitasse cups or small glasses. Cover and chill several hours or overnight.

3. Just before serving, pour a tablespoon of cream over each, if desired.

Makes 8 servings. Per serving (without cream): 167 calories, 6 grams protein, 18 grams carbohydrate, 10 grams fat, 104 milligrams cholesterol, 89 milligrams sodium

---

Melting Chocolate

☐ When melting chocolate by itself, be sure utensils are perfectly dry. As little as one small drop of water will cause chocolate to thicken into a stiff mass. If this happens, stir in a small amount of vegetable shortening (not butter, margarine or oil), about 1 teaspoon for each ounce of chocolate. However, in recipes that call for melting chocolate with liquid, the difference is in the amount of liquid. A small drop of liquid will cause the chocolate to stiffen; a larger amount (1 tablespoon per ounce) will help dissolve the sugar crystals, so the chocolate will not stiffen.

☐ Unsweetened chocolate liquefies as it melts, but semisweet, sweet cooking and milk chocolates hold their shapes until stirred.

☐ There are several methods for melting all types of chocolate:

OVER HOT WATER: Place chocolate in the top of a double boiler or in a bowl over hot, not boiling, water until almost melted. Remove top of double boiler from water. Stir chocolate until smooth.

OVER DIRECT HEAT: Place chocolate in a small heavy saucepan or skillet over very low heat. Stir constantly until smooth. Remove from heat. Chocolate scorches easily, so never increase heat to speed melting; chop or grate chocolate first if you're in a hurry.

IN MICROWAVE OVEN: Place a 1-ounce square of chocolate in a microwave-safe custard cup. Heat 1 to 2 minutes on high until almost melted, stirring once. Remove from oven and stir smooth. Increase time by about 10 seconds for each additional square.

IN OVEN: Place squares of chocolate in a small ovenproof bowl or pan over pilot light or in a warm turned-off oven.

Baked Sour Cream Chocolate Custard

Dark chocolate custard, rich with the tang of sour cream.

⅓ **cup granulated sugar**
¼ **cup unsweetened cocoa powder**
Yolks from 3 large eggs
3 **tablespoons milk**
1 **teaspoon vanilla extract**
1½ **cups sour cream**

1. Arrange one rack in the middle of the oven. Heat oven to 325°F. Have ready four 5- or 6-ounce custard cups or ramekins and an 8-inch square baking pan.

2. Stir sugar, cocoa, egg yolks, milk and vanilla in a medium-size bowl until well mixed. Stir in sour cream just until blended.

3. Pour into custard cups. Set cups in baking pan on middle oven rack. Pour enough hot water into pan to reach 1 inch up sides of cups to make a water bath.

4. Bake 35 to 40 minutes, until a thin knife inserted near the center of custards comes out clean.

5. Remove custards from water bath to a wire rack to let cool until warm. Cover and chill several hours or overnight.

6. Serve custards from cups.

Makes 4 servings. Per serving: 270 calories, 4 grams protein, 23 grams carbohydrate, 19 grams fat, 160 milligrams cholesterol, 52 milligrams sodium

Layered Chocolate-Banana Pudding

The slightly warm chocolate pudding softens the crackers.

1 **package (3⅝ ounces) chocolate**
   pudding and pie-filling mix (not
   instant pudding)
2 **cups milk or 1½ cups milk and**
   ½ **cup heavy or light cream**
1 **teaspoon vanilla extract**
8 **graham crackers (each 2½**
   inches square)
2 **medium-size bananas, sliced**
½ **cup heavy cream**
1 **tablespoon granulated sugar**
3 **tablespoons toasted sliced almonds**

1. Prepare pudding mix in a medium-size saucepan with milk according to package directions. Remove from heat. Stir in vanilla and let cool 10 minutes, stirring occasionally.

2. Arrange half the graham crackers in four dessert dishes. Spoon about half the pudding over graham crackers. Add a layer of half the bananas, then remaining crackers and bananas. Spoon remaining pudding on top. Let cool.

3. Meanwhile, whip cream with sugar with an electric mixer at high speed until cream is nearly stiff when beaters are lifted.

4. Top pudding with cream and almonds.

5. Cover and chill well before serving.

Makes 4 servings. Per serving (with milk): 428 calories, 9 grams protein, 58 grams carbohydrate, 21 grams fat, 57 milligrams cholesterol, 293 milligrams sodium

Storing Chocolate

Ideally, chocolate should be stored tightly wrapped in a relatively cool, dry place—about 60° to 70°F. At higher temperatures chocolate may acquire an unattractive pale-gray "bloom" caused by the cocoa butter's melting and rising to the surface. The bloom does not affect flavor, and the chocolate will regain its original color when melted. In a hot, humid climate, wrap chocolate tightly to prevent it from absorbing odors or moisture and store it in the refrigerator.

Fruit Puddings

Apple Raisin Pudding

A comforting dessert. Serve in bowls with half-and-half or milk.

> 4 tablespoons butter or margarine
> 4 medium-size tart apples, peeled,
>   cored and cut in 8 wedges each
> ⅓ cup raisins
> 1½ teaspoons grated fresh lemon peel
> 3 tablespoons fresh-squeezed
>   lemon juice
> 1 package (3 ounces) cream cheese,
>   at room temperature
> ½ cup granulated sugar
> 2 large eggs
> ⅔ cup all-purpose flour
> 1 cup milk

1. Turn oven to 375°F. Melt 2 tablespoons of the butter in a shallow 2-quart baking dish in oven while it heats. Remove from oven.

2. Stir apples, raisins and lemon peel and juice into melted butter and spread evenly.

3. Beat cream cheese and sugar with an electric mixer on high speed until well blended. Beat in eggs one at a time on medium speed.

4. With mixer on low speed, or with a spoon, stir flour into cream-cheese mixture in two additions, alternating with the milk, mixing just until blended. (Mixture will be slightly lumpy.)

5. Pour cream-cheese mixture over apples. Dot with remaining 2 tablespoons butter.

6. Bake 35 minutes, until a wooden pick inserted in the center comes out moist but clean. Remove from oven to a wire rack to let cool.

7. Serve pudding warm.

Makes 4 generous servings. Per serving: 541 calories, 10 grams protein, 73 grams carbohydrate, 25 grams fat, 164 milligrams cholesterol with butter, 128 milligrams cholesterol with margarine, 260 milligrams sodium

Bananas in Sauce Riche

🕐 **MAKE-AHEAD**

Bananas in Sauce Riche

If your mixer is a stationary model with two bowls, beat egg mixture in the smaller bowl, cream in the larger. Otherwise use two bowls and a portable electric mixer.

> ⅓ cup thawed frozen cholesterol-free
>   egg product
> 1 cup confectioners' sugar
> 1 tablespoon dark rum (optional)
> 1 teaspoon vanilla extract
> Pinch of salt
> 1 cup heavy cream
> 4 medium-size ripe bananas (about 1½
>   pounds), sliced ¼ inch thick
> ½ teaspoon ground nutmeg

1. Beat egg product, sugar, rum, if desired, vanilla and salt with an electric mixer on high speed about 2 minutes, until sugar is dissolved.

2. Beat cream with an electric mixer (no need to wash beaters) on high speed until soft peaks form when beaters are lifted. Gently fold egg mixture, then bananas, into cream.

3. If serving within an hour, spoon a generous ¾ cup into each of six large goblets. Sprinkle with nutmeg, cover and refrigerate.

4. If serving later, cover bowl and refrigerate. Just before serving, stir to blend (mixture will have separated).

Makes 6 servings. Per serving (with rum): 272 calories, 3 grams protein, 39 grams carbohydrate, 13 grams fat, 44 milligrams cholesterol, 60 milligrams sodium

Baked Lemon Pudding

While baking, the pudding separates into a cakelike top layer and a custard bottom. Equally good hot or at room temperature.

3 large eggs, separated
⅛ teaspoon salt
1 cup granulated sugar
½ cup milk
1 tablespoon grated fresh lemon peel
¼ cup lemon juice
¼ cup all-purpose flour
2 tablespoons margarine, melted

1. Heat oven to 350°F. Grease a deep 1½-quart casserole.

2. Beat egg whites and salt with an electric mixer at high speed until stiff peaks form when beaters are lifted.

3. Beat yolks and sugar with an electric mixer (no need to wash beaters) on high speed until thick and pale.

4. With mixer at medium speed, beat in milk, lemon peel and juice and flour until smooth.

5. Gently fold in margarine and beaten whites with a rubber spatula. Pour into prepared casserole.

6. Bake 45 minutes, until top is golden and firm to the touch. Remove from oven.

7. Serve immediately or let cool to warm and refrigerate.

Makes 4 servings. Per serving: 358 calories, 7 grams protein, 59 grams carbohydrate, 11 grams fat, 149 milligrams cholesterol, 201 milligrams sodium

🕐 **MAKE-AHEAD**

Silky Lemon Pudding

This creamy pudding is really simple to make, and it uses only one bowl. It can be prepared up to two days before serving. Lemon twists, thin slices of strawberry or fresh mint leaves make a pretty garnish instead of the chocolate.

½ cup thawed frozen cholesterol-free
  egg product
1 can (14 ounces) sweetened
  condensed milk (not
  evaporated milk)
2 teaspoons grated fresh lemon peel
½ cup fresh-squeezed lemon juice
1 cup sour cream stirred with 1
  teaspoon granulated sugar
**For garnish: 1 tablespoon grated or
  shaved semisweet chocolate**

1. Beat egg product in a medium-size bowl with a wire whisk until foamy. Whisk in sweetened condensed milk until smooth.

2. Whisk in lemon peel and juice and beat briefly until mixture thickens.

3. Spoon about ⅓ cup into each of six small wine glasses or dessert dishes. Top each with a spoonful of the sour-cream mixture. Sprinkle with chocolate.

4. Cover and refrigerate at least 1 hour before serving.

Makes 6 servings. Per serving: 323 calories, 9 grams protein, 42 grams carbohydrate, 14 grams fat, 39 milligrams cholesterol, 140 milligrams sodium

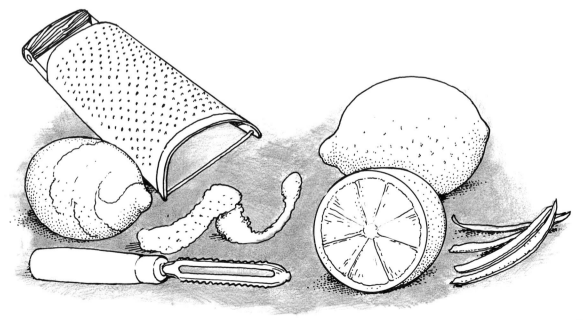

Dreamy Prune Whip

Dreamy Prune Whip

An old-fashioned dessert that's rich in flavor but not in calories. And remember, prunes are an excellent source of dietary fiber.

2 tablespoons meringue powder and
   ½ cup cold water, or whites from
   3 large eggs at room temperature
   and ¼ teaspoon cream of tartar
   (see Egg Safety, page 57)
6 tablespoons granulated sugar
8 ounces (1 packed cup) moist pitted
   prunes, snipped in small pieces
1½ tablespoons fresh-squeezed
   lemon juice
¼ teaspoon vanilla extract
Pinch of salt
¼ cup finely chopped pecans
For garnish: 16 pecan halves

1. Beat meringue powder and water (or egg whites and cream of tartar) with an electric mixer on high speed until soft peaks form when beaters are lifted. Adding 1 tablespoon sugar at a time, continue beating until whites are shiny and form stiff peaks when beaters are lifted. (If using a stationary mixer with only one bowl, gently scrape whites into a large bowl.)

2. Using the same beaters, beat prunes, lemon juice, vanilla and salt about 4 minutes until a coarse purée.

3. Fold prune mixture and chopped pecans into beaten meringue powder.

4. Spoon about ½ cup into each of eight wine glasses or dessert bowls. Cover and chill 1 hour.

5. Just before serving, garnish each dessert with 2 pecan halves.

Makes 8 servings. Per serving (with meringue powder): 128 calories, 2 grams protein, 26 grams carbohydrate, 3 grams fat, 0 milligrams cholesterol, 42 milligrams sodium

Plum Yogurt Snow
(Shown on page 87)

When fresh ripe apricots are available, try the Apricot Yogurt Snow variation, below.

- 2 **envelopes unflavored gelatin**
- ¾ **cup cold water**
- 1¾ **pounds ripe purple or red plums (about 8 medium-size), halved, pitted and cut in wedges**
- ½ **cup granulated sugar**
- ¼ **cup plum preserves**
- ⅓ **cup plain low-fat yogurt**
- 1 **tablespoon meringue powder and ¼ cup cold water, or whites from 2 large eggs at room temperature and ¼ teaspoon cream of tartar (see Egg Safety, page 57)**

For garnish: additional plain low-fat yogurt

1. Sprinkle gelatin over ½ cup of the cold water in a small bowl. Let stand 2 minutes to soften.

2. Mix plums, ¼ cup of the sugar, the preserves and ¼ cup water in a medium-size saucepan. Bring to a boil over medium heat, stirring often to break up fruit. Remove from heat.

3. Add gelatin mixture to plums and stir about 3 minutes, until completely dissolved. Let cool 5 minutes. Stir in yogurt.

4. Process plum mixture, in batches if necessary, in a food processor or a blender until smooth.

5. Pour purée into a medium-size bowl. Refrigerate about 1½ hours, stirring three times, until mixture thickens to the consistency of unbeaten egg whites and mounds when dropped from a spoon.

6. Beat meringue powder and water (or egg whites and cream of tartar) with an electric mixer at high speed until foamy. Gradually add remaining ¼ cup sugar and beat until stiff peaks form when beaters are lifted. Fold into plum mixture.

7. Spoon into six wine glasses or a 1½-quart serving bowl, cover loosely and chill about 2 hours, until set. Garnish with dollops of yogurt and serve.

Makes 6 servings. Per serving (with meringue powder): 182 calories, 4 grams protein, 43 grams carbohydrate, 0 grams fat, 1 milligram cholesterol, 36 milligrams sodium

Variation: For Apricot Yogurt Snow, substitute 1¾ pounds ripe apricots for the plums, and apricot preserves for the plum preserves. Proceed as directed.

Rhubarb Snow

Rhubarb has a short season—February to May—but it is easy to freeze, so you can always have some on hand. Just trim leaves off stalks, wash well and cut in pieces. Pack in freezer bags or containers and freeze. Remember: Rhubarb leaves are poisonous.

- 3 **cups 1-inch pieces fresh rhubarb or 1 bag (16 ounces) frozen rhubarb (no need to thaw)**
- ½ **cup water**
- 1 **package (3 ounces) strawberry-flavor gelatin**
- 1 **cup ice cubes**
- 2 **tablespoons meringue powder and ½ cup cold water, or whites from 3 large eggs, at room temperature (see Egg Safety, page 57)**
- 1 **tablespoon granulated sugar**

1. Bring rhubarb and water to a boil in a medium-size saucepan (not uncoated aluminum). Reduce heat to low. Cover and simmer 10 minutes, stirring occasionally, until tender. Remove from heat.

2. Add gelatin to rhubarb and stir about 1 minute, until gelatin is completely dissolved.

3. Pour into a food processor or a blender. Process 15 seconds, until smooth. Add ice cubes and process until ice has melted.

4. Pour mixture into a large bowl and refrigerate 10 minutes, stirring occasionally, until cool.

5. Meanwhile, beat meringue powder and water (or egg whites) with an electric mixer on high speed until soft peaks form when beaters are lifted. Add sugar and beat until stiff peaks form.

6. Stir about one third of the beaten meringue powder into the rhubarb purée until well blended. Gently fold in remaining meringue powder.

7. Spoon into four dessert glasses or a medium-size serving bowl. Chill about 1 hour, until set. Serve. (Some separation of purée and egg-white mixture may occur in bottom of dish.)

Makes 4 servings. Per serving (with meringue powder): 116 calories, 5 grams protein, 25 grams carbohydrate, 0 grams fat, 0 milligrams cholesterol, 106 milligrams sodium

Iced Raspberry Zabaglione

A refreshingly flavorful dessert. One of Italy's culinary masterpieces, zabaglione is made by whisking egg yolks, sugar and, traditionally, marsala wine into a light, foamy custard.

Yolks from 6 large eggs
7 tablespoons granulated sugar
½ cup water
6 tablespoons gold (medium) rum
Seeds scraped from a split 5-inch
    vanilla bean (see Vanilla, page 61)
About ¾ cup fresh raspberries, rinsed
    and drained
½ cup heavy cream
Scant ½ teaspoon vanilla extract

1. Beat egg yolks, 6 tablespoons of the sugar, the water, rum and vanilla seeds in the top of a double boiler with a wire whisk or a rotary beater.

2. Place over simmering water on low heat. Cook 5 to 10 minutes, whisking or beating constantly, until mixture is thick, light, smooth, increased in volume and a candy or instant-read thermometer registers 160°F. Remove from heat.

3. Set top of double boiler in a bowl of ice cubes, whisking zabaglione occasionally until cooled.

4. Pour zabaglione into six small stemmed glasses, wide-bowl wine glasses or small berry bowls. Cover and refrigerate until thoroughly chilled.

5. Top each portion with some of the raspberries.

6. With an electric mixer at high speed, beat cream with remaining 1 tablespoon sugar and the vanilla until soft peaks form when beaters are lifted. Pass whipped cream in a bowl or dollop a small spoonful on each portion and serve.

Makes 6 servings. Per serving: 191 calories, 3 grams protein, 17 grams carbohydrate, 13 grams fat, 217 milligrams cholesterol, 15 milligrams sodium

Ricotta Pudding with Berry Sauce

A red, white and blue dessert perfect to serve on the Fourth of July. You can make the pudding in a blender instead of a food processor, but it will have a thinner, saucelike consistency.

RICOTTA PUDDING

¼ cup granulated sugar
3-inch-long strip lemon peel, removed
    with a vegetable peeler
½ cup heavy cream
1 container (15 ounces) ricotta cheese
1 package (3 ounces) cream cheese, at
    room temperature

BERRY SAUCE

2 cups fresh strawberries, rinsed,
    drained and hulled
2 tablespoons granulated sugar
1 tablespoon water
2 teaspoons fresh-squeezed
    lemon juice
2 cups fresh raspberries, rinsed
    and drained
2 cups fresh blueberries, rinsed
    and drained

1. To make ricotta pudding: Pour sugar into a food processor. Turn machine on and drop lemon peel through feed tube. Process until peel is finely chopped, turning off processor once or twice to scrape down sides.

2. Pour cream through feed tube. Process until blended. Add cheeses and process about 2 minutes, until very smooth, turning off processor once to scrape down sides.

3. Scrape pudding into a medium-size serving bowl or spoon into eight wine glasses. Cover and chill at least 4 hours or overnight.

4. To make berry sauce: Process strawberries, sugar, water and lemon juice in a food processor or a blender until very smooth.

5. Pour sauce into a medium-size bowl. Gently stir in raspberries and blueberries. Taste sauce; add more sugar or lemon juice, if desired. Cover and chill until serving time or spoon the sauce over pudding and serve immediately.

Makes 8 servings. Per serving: 274 calories, 8 grams protein, 24 grams carbohydrate, 17 grams fat, 59 milligrams cholesterol, 78 milligrams sodium

Custards

⏱ **MAKE-AHEAD**
✳ **MICROWAVE**

Basic Baked Custard

2 cups milk
3 large eggs
⅓ cup granulated sugar
1 teaspoon vanilla extract
⅛ teaspoon salt
Ground cinnamon or nutmeg (optional)

1. Arrange one rack in the middle of the oven. Heat oven to 325°F. Have ready four 6-ounce custard cups set in a 13x9-inch baking dish.

2. Heat milk in a small heavy saucepan over medium heat just until small bubbles form around the edges. Remove from heat.

3. Beat eggs, sugar, vanilla and salt in a medium-size bowl with a wire whisk until well blended. Whisking constantly, gradually beat in hot milk.

4. Strain through a strainer into a large glass measure for easy handling. Pour into custard cups.

5. Put baking pan on middle oven rack. Pour enough hot water into pan to reach 1 inch up sides of custard cups to make a water bath.

6. Bake 30 minutes, until a thin knife inserted near centers of custards comes out clean. Remove cups from water bath to a wire rack to let cool until warm.

7. Serve warm or cover and chill until ready to serve. Just before serving, sprinkle lightly with cinnamon, if desired.

Makes 4 servings. Per serving: 205 calories, 9 grams protein, 23 grams carbohydrate, 9 grams fat, 151 milligrams cholesterol, 176 milligrams sodium

Microwave Method: Heat milk in a 2-cup microwave-safe glass measure on medium-high about 4 minutes, until hot but not boiling. Assemble custard as directed. Pour into microwave-safe custard cups. Arrange in oven in a circle. Cook on medium 5 minutes; rotate and rearrange cups. Cook 3 to 5 minutes longer, until custard is set near the edges. Remove to a heatproof surface to let cool to warm. Proceed as directed.

Creating Perfect Custards

☐ A custard is a mixture of eggs and milk and/or cream. It may be cooked on top of the stove (called a stirred custard) or baked in the oven. The milk is often scalded to reduce overall cooking time and to produce a smoother result. Scalding milk means heating it only until tiny bubbles form around the edges; it can be done in a heavy saucepan over low-to-medium heat or in a microwave-safe container in a microwave oven on high.

BAKED CUSTARDS: Pour the mixture for a baked custard into heatproof glass, ceramic or china baking cups or baking dishes. Set the filled cups in a baking pan large enough so that the custard cups don't touch. Add hot water to the baking pan as directed in recipe to make a water bath. Custards are baked in a water bath so that they cook slowly and evenly. Overbaking produces a watery custard. Custard is done when it wiggles slightly in the center and a thin knife inserted off-center comes out clean. It will continue to cook as it cools.

STIRRED CUSTARDS: Since custard may curdle when cooked over direct heat, cooking stirred custard in a double boiler is helpful for the less-experienced cook. If you don't have a double boiler, you can easily devise one by setting a saucepan over a large saucepan or in a skillet filled with hot water. To cook custard over direct heat, place a heavy-bottomed saucepan over low heat. Using a figure-eight motion, stir with a wooden spoon just until mixture is thickened and coats a metal spoon and a candy or instant-read thermometer registers 160°F. If custard overcooks and curdles slightly (it acquires a grainy look), remove from heat immediately and beat smooth with a whisk or a rotary beater, then strain it through a fine strainer. Cool stirred custard quickly by placing the saucepan in a bowl of ice water. Add flavoring. Transfer to a serving dish and cover and chill until ready to use.

Mexican Flan

A microwave version of a favorite dessert.

½ **cup granulated sugar**
2 **tablespoons water**
4 **large eggs**
1 **can (14 ounces) sweetened**
    condensed milk
1 **can (12 ounces) evaporated milk**
⅓ **cup half-and-half or milk**
2 **tablespoons brandy or 2 teaspoons**
    brandy flavoring
2 **teaspoons vanilla extract**
1 **teaspoon instant coffee powder**
    (not granules)

1. Have ready six 6-ounce microwave-safe glass custard cups.

2. Mix sugar and water in a 2-cup glass measure (not plastic). Microwave on high 5½ to 7½ minutes, until mixture boils and turns a walnut-brown color. Watch carefully toward the end of minimum cooking time to prevent burning.

3. Working quickly, pour caramel evenly into bottoms of cups.

4. Whisk eggs in a large bowl. Whisk in sweetened condensed milk, evaporated milk, half-and-half, brandy, vanilla and coffee powder until well blended.

5. Pour egg mixture into a large glass measure or pitcher for easier handling and pour evenly into prepared custard cups.

6. Arrange cups in a circle in microwave oven. Microwave on medium 13 to 18 minutes, rotating cups ¼ turn every 4 minutes. Custard is done when a thin knife comes out clean when inserted near edges but thickly coated when inserted in centers. Centers will firm up upon standing and chilling. Let cool on countertop 30 minutes.

7. Refrigerate a minimum of 4 hours before unmolding.

8. To unmold: Run a thin knife between flan and edges of cups to loosen. Invert onto dessert plates and serve.

Makes 6 servings. Per serving (with half-and-half and brandy): 515 calories, 16 grams protein, 72 grams carbohydrate, 18 grams fat, 184 milligrams cholesterol, 221 milligrams sodium

Egg Safety

☐ IT IS EXTREMELY IMPORTANT TO THOROUGHLY COOK EGGS AND EGG-RICH FOODS to minimize the risk from any harmful bacteria such as salmonella that may be present (especially dangerous for children and the elderly). This means you must cook custards and bases for ice creams to a temperature of 160°F to ensure a wholesome result. Baked custards and puddings may be considered safe, especially if you eat or refrigerate them soon after baking.

☐ Avoid making desserts with raw eggs, especially egg yolks. Instead, follow recipe directions for using cholesterol-free egg products (such as Egg Beaters), which are pasteurized and so require no cooking for health reasons.

☐ Because of the small but very real chance of salmonella contamination from raw egg whites, *Woman's Day* strongly recommends you use meringue powder made from pasteurized dried egg whites, sugar and food starch, as directed in the recipes, instead of fresh egg whites. However, should you wish to use fresh egg whites, these directions are also included. Meringue powder can be purchased from cake-decorating-supply stores or ordered by mail. Write to Maid of Scandinavia, 3244 Raleigh Avenue, Minneapolis, MN 55416, or call toll-free 1-800-328-6722 (in Minnesota, 1-800-851-1121; Twin Cities metro area, call 925-9256). Or write to Wilton Enterprises, Inc., 2240 West 75th Street, Woodridge, IL 60517; or call toll-free 1-800-772-7111 (963-7100 in the Woodridge area) and ask for mail-order.

On-a-Diet Crème Caramel

CARAMEL

½ cup granulated sugar
¼ cup water

CUSTARD

2½ cups skim milk
½ cup nonfat dry-milk powder
3 large eggs
Whites from 3 large eggs
2 tablespoons granulated sugar
1 teaspoon vanilla extract
5 drops yellow food coloring
   (optional)

1. Have ready a 4-cup soufflé dish or charlotte mold and a 13x9-inch baking pan.

2. To make caramel: Mix sugar and water in a small heavy saucepan. Bring to a boil over medium heat. Boil without stirring (stirring causes granules to form) 5 to 10 minutes, until sugar dissolves completely and syrup is straw-colored. Raise heat to medium-high and boil 2 minutes longer, until syrup is amber-colored. (Watch carefully or syrup may blacken and burn.)

3. Immediately pour syrup into soufflé dish. Using oven mitts or pot holders, pick up dish and tilt carefully to coat bottom and sides. Let cool to room temperature.

4. To make custard: Heat oven to 325°F. Heat milk in a medium-size saucepan over low heat just until small bubbles appear around the edges. Remove from heat and stir in dry-milk powder until completely dissolved.

5. Whisk eggs, egg whites, sugar, vanilla and food coloring, if desired, in a medium-size bowl until well blended. Beating constantly, gradually pour in hot milk.

6. Strain mixture through a fine strainer into prepared dish. Place dish in baking pan and pour enough hot water into pan to reach halfway up side of dish to make a water bath.

7. Bake 1 hour and 15 minutes, until a thin knife inserted near the center of custard comes out clean. Remove custard from water bath to a wire rack. Let cool until warm, then refrigerate at least 2 hours before unmolding and serving.

8. To unmold: Run a thin knife around inside edge of dish to partially release custard. Invert serving plate over dish, turn both over together, then shake dish gently and lift off.

9. Serve immediately or refrigerate until ready to serve.

Makes 6 servings. Per serving: 182 calories, 5 grams protein, 28 grams carbohydrate, 3 grams fat, 100 milligrams cholesterol, 25 milligrams sodium

Baked Custards with Jelly Syrup
(Shown on page 46)

Although inspired by the classic caramel custard or flan, this very pretty dessert does not require any sugar-carmelizing.

1¾ cups milk
¼ cup red-currant jelly
3 large eggs
⅓ cup granulated sugar
1 teaspoon vanilla extract
⅛ teaspoon salt

1. Arrange one rack in the middle of the oven. Heat oven to 325°F. Grease four 6-ounce custard cups or ramekins. Have ready a shallow 13x9-inch baking pan.

2. Heat milk in a small saucepan over medium heat just until small bubbles form around the edges. Remove from heat.

3. Stir jelly until thin. Spoon 1 teaspoon into each prepared custard cup. Reserve remaining jelly.

4. Beat eggs, sugar, vanilla and salt in a large bowl just until blended. Gradually whisk in hot milk. Strain mixture through a fine strainer into a large glass measure. Pour into custard cups.

5. Place custard cups in baking pan. Place pan on middle oven rack. Pour enough hot water into baking pan to reach 1 inch up sides of custard cups to make a water bath.

6. Bake 30 minutes, until a thin knife inserted near centers of custards comes out clean. Remove cups to a wire rack. Let cool until warm, then chill at least 1 hour.

7. To unmold: Run a knife around custards to loosen and invert onto serving plates. Melt remaining jelly in a small skillet or saucepan over low heat.

8. Spoon melted jelly over custards and serve immediately.

Makes 4 servings. Per serving: 246 calories, 9 grams protein, 35 grams carbohydrate, 8 grams fat, 151 milligrams cholesterol, 172 milligrams sodium

Raspberry Custard

This exquisite custard can be made up to four days ahead.

---

    3 tablespoons seedless red-raspberry jam
    2 teaspoons plus ½ cup granulated sugar
1¼ cups fresh raspberries
    3 large eggs
Yolks from 3 large eggs
    1 teaspoon vanilla extract
    2 cups (1 pint) heavy cream
    ½ cup milk

1. Arrange one rack in the middle of the oven. Heat oven to 325°F. Put eight 6-ounce ramekins or custard cups in a baking pan just large enough to hold them.

2. Stir jam and 2 teaspoons of the sugar in a medium-size bowl until blended. Add berries and fold in gently to coat. Spoon into ramekins.

3. Whisk eggs, egg yolks, vanilla and remaining ½ cup sugar in a large bowl until thoroughly blended. Whisk in cream and milk.

4. Pour egg mixture into a large glass measure or pitcher for easier handling and pour evenly into ramekins.

5. Place pan on middle oven rack. Pour enough hot water into baking pan to reach about one third up sides of ramekins to make a water bath.

6. Bake 45 to 50 minutes, until a thin knife inserted near centers of custards comes out clean. Place pan on a wire rack. Leave ramekins in water bath 10 minutes (they will continue to cook).

7. Remove ramekins from water bath to rack to let cool until warm. Cover and refrigerate until cold, at least 2 hours. Serve in ramekins.

Makes 8 servings. Per serving: 352 calories, 6 grams protein, 23 grams carbohydrate, 27 grams fat, 247 milligrams cholesterol, 54 milligrams sodium

Microwave Method: Prepare berries and custard as directed. Assemble in microwave-safe ramekins (no metal trim) or custard cups. In microwave oven, arrange 4 ramekins in a square, with about 2 inches between each. Microwave on medium 8 to 10 minutes, rotating ramekins ½ turn and rearranging them every 3 minutes. Custard is done when a thin knife inserted near edges comes out clean but is thickly coated when inserted in centers. Remove from oven and let stand 30 minutes to cool. Centers will firm on standing. Repeat with remaining custards. Chill as directed.

Custard Cups and Ramekins

☐ Ramekins are individual straight-sided baking dishes, usually with a capacity of 6 to 8 ounces. Made of porcelain, they resemble tiny soufflé dishes and go with ease from oven, broiler or microwave to table, refrigerator or freezer.

☐ Ramekins are usually white, but pretty decorative versions are available. They are also available gold-painted or with gold rims, which unless otherwise stated are not suitable for microwave cooking.

☐ Custard cups have curved sides and come in a variety of sizes, but 6 ounces is the standard. They are made from porcelain, earthenware or glass. All these materials are ovenproof (but check the bottom or the box they came in just to be sure) and are suitable for conventional or microwave baking. Custards may also be baked in coffee cups or teacups, especially decorative ones, but be sure that they are ovenproof.

Raspberry Custard

Basic Stirred Custard

A creamy dessert or a topping for fruit or cake, this custard can also be used as a base for other desserts.

2 cups milk or half-and-half
3 large eggs
¼ cup granulated sugar
⅛ teaspoon salt
1 teaspoon vanilla extract or
     1 tablespoon sherry or rum,
     or to taste

1. Heat milk in a medium-size heavy saucepan over medium heat just until small bubbles form around the edges. Remove from heat.

2. Beat eggs, sugar and salt in a medium-size bowl with a wire whisk until well blended. Whisking constantly, gradually beat in hot milk.

3. Return mixture to saucepan. Cook over low heat about 8 minutes, stirring constantly, until custard is slightly thickened, coats a metal spoon and registers 160°F on a candy or instant-read thermometer.

4. Immediately set saucepan in a bowl of ice water to let cool. Stir in vanilla.

5. Pour custard into a serving bowl; cover and chill until ready to serve.

Makes 4 dessert or 8 sauce servings. Per dessert serving (with milk and vanilla extract): 182 calories, 9 grams protein, 19 grams carbohydrate, 8 grams fat, 161 milligrams cholesterol, 176 milligrams sodium

Microwave Method: Heat milk in a 2-cup microwave-safe glass measure on medium-high about 4 minutes, until hot but not boiling. Assemble custard as directed in a 1-quart microwave-safe casserole. Cook on medium-high 5 to 7 minutes, stirring at least twice, until custard is thickened, coats a metal spoon and registers 160°F on a candy or instant-read thermometer. Proceed as directed.

Custard with Strawberries

Yolks from 4 large eggs
¼ cup plus 1 tablespoon
     granulated sugar
¼ teaspoon freshly grated or
     ground nutmeg
⅛ teaspoon salt
1¼ cups milk
½ teaspoon vanilla extract
1 pint basket strawberries, rinsed,
     drained and hulled (about 3 cups)
2 tablespoons lightly toasted sliced
     almonds

1. Whisk egg yolks, ¼ cup of the sugar, the nutmeg and salt in a medium-size heavy saucepan (preferably stainless or enamelware). Stir in milk.

2. Stir constantly over low heat until mixture thickens slightly, coats a metal spoon and registers 160°F on a candy or instant-read thermometer. Remove from heat and stir in vanilla.

3. Let custard cool until warm, stirring occasionally. Pour into four wine glasses or small dessert dishes. Cover loosely and chill several hours or overnight.

4. Just before serving, top custards with strawberries. Mix almonds and remaining 1 tablespoon sugar in a cup and sprinkle over custards.

Makes 4 servings. Per serving: 220 calories, 7 grams protein, 26 grams carbohydrate, 10 grams fat, 202 milligrams cholesterol, 115 milligrams sodium

Caramel-Glazed Banana Custard

This rich fruit-filled custard is a simplified version of crème brûlée. Custard may be made up to two days ahead. The caramel glaze keeps at least two weeks. Any leftover caramel may be served cold over sliced fruit.

CUSTARD

¼ **cup granulated sugar**
2 **teaspoons cornstarch**
1 **large egg**
1 **cup milk**
¼ **teaspoon vanilla extract**

CARAMEL GLAZE AND FRUIT

1 **cup granulated sugar**
¾ **cup water**
¼ **cup heavy cream, at room temperature**
1 **tablespoon apple-cider vinegar**
5 **medium-size bananas (about 1¾ pounds)**

1. To make custard: Mix sugar and cornstarch in a medium-size bowl. Add egg and whisk until smooth.

2. Bring milk to a boil in a medium-size saucepan. Remove from heat.

3. Slowly whisk hot milk into egg mixture, then return mixture to saucepan. Cook over medium heat 2 to 2½ minutes, stirring constantly, until custard thickens, coats a metal spoon and registers 160°F on a candy or instant-read thermometer. Remove from heat and stir in vanilla.

4. Pour custard into a bowl. Cover surface with plastic wrap to prevent skin from forming. Refrigerate until completely cool, 1 to 2 hours or up to 2 days.

5. To make caramel glaze: Stir sugar and ½ cup of the water in a medium-size saucepan over medium heat until sugar is dissolved. Increase heat to medium-high and bring to a boil. Boil without stirring 9 to 10 minutes, until syrup starts to darken around edges (stirring may cause sugar crystals to form). Shake pan gently to blend colors. When syrup is a medium-copper color, remove saucepan from heat.

6. Cover saucepan with a fine flat sieve or spatter screen to prevent splattering (caramel is very hot). Carefully pour remaining ¼ cup water and the cream through the sieve. Remove sieve and shake pan gently to mix. Caramel mixture may glob in center. If it does, place saucepan over medium heat and stir until mixture dissolves. Stir in vinegar. (At this point, caramel may be scraped into a bowl, covered and chilled for up to 2 weeks. Heat over low heat before serving.)

7. To serve: Peel bananas and cut in ½-inch-thick rounds. Fold into chilled custard. Spoon into six sherbet or wine glasses. Top each with a tablespoonful of warm caramel sauce. Serve immediately.

Makes 6 servings and about 1 cup caramel sauce. Per serving (with 1 tablespoon sauce): 258 calories, 4 grams protein, 55 grams carbohydrate, 5 grams fat, 51 milligrams cholesterol, 34 milligrams sodium

---

Vanilla

☐ Vanilla is the most popular ice-cream flavor in the United States and one of the most popular flavorings in desserts. Since it's so commonly used, we think of it as a plain flavor, yet it is actually a very complex natural flavor produced under a process as labor-intensive and time-consuming as wine making.

☐ Vanilla, the fruit of an exotic tropical orchid, is sold both as whole beans and as liquid extract. Always buy pure, not imitation, vanilla extract, as the latter will not have the same delicate perfume and rich flavor.

☐ The whole vanilla bean is sold in jars on the spice racks in supermarkets and in specialty shops. Vanilla beans are expensive, but the seeds impart an exotic full flavor to desserts. You can bury a whole bean in your sugar canister to make vanilla sugar; scald the milk for a custard with a halved bean in it; or scrape out the seeds to add to whipped cream or ice cream. After using, the whole bean or the halves can be rinsed and dried to use once or twice again, or until the bean is no longer fragrant.

Rice Puddings

🕐 **MAKE-AHEAD**
✳ **MICROWAVE**

Rich Rice Pudding with Lingonberries

A quick recipe for busy people. This is a Swedish Christmas Eve favorite, and tradition holds that whoever gets the almond will be the next to marry.

3 cups milk
⅔ cup 5-minute rice
3 large eggs
⅔ cup granulated sugar
1 teaspoon vanilla extract
½ teaspoon salt
½ teaspoon ground nutmeg
1 whole blanched almond
For garnish: ½ cup whole lingonberries in sugar (from a jar; see Note) or canned whole-berry cranberry sauce

1. Heat oven to 375°F. Have ready a deep 1½-quart baking dish and a shallow baking pan.

2. Bring milk to a boil in a medium-size saucepan. Remove from heat and stir in rice.

3. Whisk eggs in a medium-size bowl. Stir in sugar, vanilla, salt and nutmeg.

4. Gradually add hot milk-rice mixture to eggs, whisking constantly, until blended.

5. Pour rice mixture into baking dish. Put baking dish in baking pan. Place pan on oven rack and pour enough hot water into pan to reach halfway up side of dish to make a water bath.

6. Bake 20 minutes, stirring twice to distribute rice evenly, then add blanched almond.

7. Bake 20 to 25 minutes longer, until a thin knife inserted in the center comes out clean. Remove baking dish from water bath to a wire rack and let cool until warm.

8. Serve warm or chill and serve cold. Just before serving, spoon lingonberries over top.

Makes 4 cups, 8 servings. Per ½ cup (without lingonberries): 183 calories, 6 grams protein, 28 grams carbohydrate, 5 grams fat, 62 milligrams cholesterol, 202 milligrams sodium

Note: Lingonberries in sugar, similar to a jam, are sold in specialty stores and supermarket gourmet sections.

Microwave Method: Microwave milk in a deep 3-quart microwave-safe casserole on high 8 to 10 minutes, until boiling. Stir in rice. Meanwhile, assemble egg mixture as directed above. Stir about ¼ cup of the hot milk-rice mixture into eggs, then whisk eggs into remaining milk-rice mixture. Cover tightly with a lid or vented plastic wrap. Microwave on medium 3 minutes; stir in almond. Microwave covered 3 to 5 minutes longer, stirring once, until edges are set and center jiggles when dish is gently shaken. Let stand 15 to 20 minutes, until center is set.

Rich Rice Pudding with Lingonberries

Custardy Rice Pudding

(Shown on page 64)

All the pleasure with none of the guilt in this dessert that uses skim milk instead of cream and cuts back the sugar.

 2 **cups skim milk**
 ½ **cup thawed frozen cholesterol-free egg product**
 ¼ **cup granulated sugar**
 1 **tablespoon cornstarch**
 2 **teaspoons vanilla extract**
 1 **strip fresh orange peel (about 2 inches long), removed with a vegetable peeler**
 2 **cups cooked white rice**
Ground nutmeg

1. Heat milk in a medium-size saucepan over medium heat until very warm.

2. Meanwhile, mix egg product, sugar, cornstarch and vanilla in a 2-cup measure or a small bowl until blended and smooth.

3. Add orange peel to the warmed milk, then gradually stir in the egg mixture. Cook 2 to 3 minutes, stirring frequently, until mixture comes to a boil. Boil 1 minute, stirring constantly.

4. Remove peel from milk mixture and discard. Stir in rice and remove from heat.

5. Pour pudding into a medium-size serving bowl. Let cool until warm, then cover surface with plastic wrap. Chill at least 3 hours or up to 2 days.

6. Just before serving, sprinkle with nutmeg.

Makes 8 servings, ½ cup each. Per serving: 99 calories, 4 grams protein, 20 grams carbohydrate, less than ¼ gram fat, 1 milligram cholesterol, 52 milligrams sodium

---

Raisins

☐ Raisins are grapes that have been dried in the sun. Golden raisins are dried grapes treated with sulfur dioxide, which retains their natural golden color and gives them a tangy flavor.

☐ Raisins add natural sweetness to desserts, and they also help to keep baked goods moist.

☐ Once opened, store raisins in an airtight container in the refrigerator to keep them soft.

Rice Pudding with Raisins

⏱ MAKE-AHEAD

Rice Pudding with Raisins

Good for dessert and for breakfast, too.

 1 **quart (4 cups) 1%-fat milk**
 ½ **cup uncooked long-grain white rice**
 ½ **cup raisins**
 1 **large egg**
Whites from 2 large eggs
 ⅓ **cup granulated sugar**
 1 **cup evaporated skim milk**
 1½ **teaspoons vanilla extract**
Ground nutmeg

1. Put milk, rice and raisins in a large heavy saucepan or Dutch oven and bring to a boil over medium-high heat. Reduce heat to low and simmer 20 minutes, stirring often, until rice is almost tender.

2. Meanwhile, whisk egg, egg whites, sugar and evaporated milk in a medium-size bowl until blended. Stirring constantly, gradually add to hot rice mixture. Stir over low heat about 3 minutes, until slightly thickened. Remove from heat and stir in vanilla.

3. Pour pudding into a shallow serving dish or individual dessert glasses. Serve warm or cover and chill until ready to serve.

4. Just before serving, sprinkle with nutmeg.

Makes about 4½ cups. Per ½ cup: 190 calories, 9 grams protein, 34 grams carbohydrate, 2 grams fat, 15 milligrams cholesterol, 122 milligrams sodium

Bread Puddings

German Lemon Bread Pudding

A custardy sauce forms underneath.

6 tablespoons butter or margarine
1½ cups fine crumbs from day-old French or Italian bread (not sourdough) or firm white bread
2 large eggs
Yolk from 1 large egg
¾ cup plus 2 teaspoons granulated sugar
1½ cups milk
2 teaspoons grated fresh lemon peel
½ teaspoon vanilla extract
⅛ teaspoon salt
Heavy cream (optional)

1. Heat oven to 350°F. Grease a 1-quart soufflé dish or baking dish. Have a shallow baking pan ready.

2. Melt butter in a heavy skillet over medium heat. Add crumbs and stir until crisp and deep golden brown. Remove skillet from heat.

3. Lightly beat eggs and egg yolk in a medium-size bowl. Beat in ¾ cup of the sugar, the milk, lemon peel, vanilla and salt. Stir in crumbs.

4. Pour mixture into prepared dish. Place dish in baking pan. Pour enough hot water into pan to reach 1 inch up side of dish to make a water bath. Sprinkle surface of pudding with remaining 2 teaspoons sugar.

5. Bake 50 minutes, until a thin knife inserted near the center comes out clean. Remove from water bath to a wire rack. Let cool until warm.

6. Serve with heavy cream, if desired.

Makes 5 servings. Per serving (without cream): 374 calories, 7 grams protein, 42 grams carbohydrate, 20 grams fat, 169 milligrams cholesterol with butter, 126 milligrams cholesterol with margarine, 354 milligrams sodium

---

Bread Pudding

☐ Making a bread pudding is a time-honored way to turn stale bread into something delicious. Today's plastic-wrapped breads rarely dry out, so you may need to create your own "stale" or dry bread. Here's an explanation of the various forms called for in our recipes:

DAY-OLD BREAD: Leave bread unwrapped or in an open paper bag to dehydrate a little.

SOFT BREAD CRUMBS: Tear or crumble fresh or day-old bread into very small pieces. Or put chunks of bread in a blender or a food processor and process until coarse or fine, as desired.

DRY BREAD CRUMBS: Either allow fresh bread crumbs to dehydrate uncovered at room temperature (or in a 200°F oven) until crisp and dry, or break up bread that is already hard and dry (most Italian and French breads will dry out overnight).

☐ Three ways to reduce bread to crumbs:

1. Processing in a blender or a food processor.

2. Pressing it through the fine blade of a food grinder.

3. Crushing pieces in a plastic bag with a rolling pin (bread points will pierce bag, so break into small pieces first).

Clockwise from top right: Slim Chocolate Mousse, Slim Banana Split, Custardy Rice Pudding

Coach House Bread Pudding with Raspberry Sauce

(Shown on page 46)

This pudding was inspired by the famous New York City Coach House restaurant.

- 1 long loaf (8 ounces) day-old French or Italian bread (not sourdough), cut in ½-inch slices, or 8 slices firm white bread, crusts removed
- ¼ cup butter or margarine, at room temperature
- 4 large eggs

Yolks from 2 large eggs
- ¾ cup granulated sugar
- 1½ teaspoons vanilla extract
- ½ teaspoon ground cinnamon
- ¼ teaspoon ground nutmeg
- ⅛ teaspoon salt
- 3 cups milk
- ⅔ cup heavy cream
- 2 tablespoons confectioners' sugar

Raspberry Sauce (recipe follows)
Lightly whipped cream (optional)

1. Heat oven to 375°F. Grease a shallow 2-quart baking dish or soufflé dish. Have a shallow baking pan ready.

2. Spread one side of bread slices with butter. Layer slices buttered-side up in baking dish.

3. Whisk eggs, egg yolks, granulated sugar, vanilla, cinnamon, nutmeg and salt in a large bowl.

4. Heat milk and cream in a medium-size saucepan just until small bubbles form around the edges. Gradually beat into egg mixture. Pour over the bread. (Bread will float to the top.)

5. Place baking dish in shallow baking pan. Pour enough hot water into pan to reach 1 inch up side of dish to make a water bath. Bake 45 to 50 minutes, until a thin knife inserted near the center comes out clean. Remove from water bath to a wire rack. Let cool until warm.

6. Dust top of pudding with confectioners' sugar. Put under broiler for 1 minute, until sugar melts and glazes.

7. To serve: Spoon some Raspberry Sauce on each plate, put a serving of pudding in the center and top with dollop of whipped cream, if desired.

Makes 8 generous servings. Per serving (without sauce or cream): 398 calories, 10 grams protein, 42 grams carbohydrate, 20 grams fat, 231 milligrams cholesterol with butter, 213 milligrams cholesterol with margarine, 356 milligrams sodium

Raspberry Sauce

- 2 packages (10 ounces each) thawed frozen raspberries in syrup
- ½ cup water
- 1 tablespoon cornstarch
- 1 tablespoon lemon juice

1. Put raspberries in a food processor or a blender and purée until smooth.

2. Mix water and cornstarch in a medium-size saucepan. Press purée through a strainer suspended over the saucepan to remove seeds; discard seeds.

3. Place saucepan over medium heat and bring just to a boil, stirring constantly, until sauce thickens. Boil 1 minute. Remove from heat and stir in lemon juice.

4. Serve warm or chill and reheat until warm before serving.

Makes 1¾ cups. Per 2 tablespoons: 42 calories, 0 grams protein, 11 grams carbohydrate, 0 grams fat, 0 milligrams cholesterol, 0 milligrams sodium

---

Folding in Egg Whites

This technique is used for soufflés, mousses and other desserts with light, airy textures. It's also used for beaten meringue powder and whipped cream—anytime a recipe tells you to fold mixtures together. The tools you'll need are a large bowl and, for best results, a large rubber spatula. Starting at the side farthest away from you, cut down vertically with the rubber spatula through the two mixtures, across the bottom of the bowl and up the nearest side. Rotate the bowl one quarter turn with each stroke, until the mixtures are combined yet still fluffy, with no volume lost. Sometimes mixtures will not incorporate completely; follow recipe instructions.

★ SPECIAL—AND WORTH IT
Swiss Chocolate Pudding

This separates in baking—a soft custard sauce below, soft crumbs on top. The egg whites will not fold completely into the chocolate mixture, but you should follow the folding technique (see Folding in Egg Whites, page 66); you'll lose volume if you stir.

- 2 squares (1 ounce each) unsweetened chocolate
- ⅓ cup butter or margarine
- 3 large eggs (separate 2)
- 1¼ cups granulated sugar
- ⅛ teaspoon salt
- ½ teaspoon vanilla extract
- 1½ cups milk
- 1½ cups fine soft crumbs from day-old French or Italian bread (not sourdough) or firm white bread
- 1 teaspoon confectioners' sugar
- 1 cup heavy cream

1. Heat oven to 350°F. Grease a 1½-quart soufflé dish or baking dish. Have a shallow baking pan ready.

2. Melt chocolate and butter in a small heavy saucepan over low heat. Remove from heat and let cool.

3. Beat 1 whole egg and 2 egg yolks in a medium-size bowl until blended. Then beat in, in the following order, 1 cup of the granulated sugar, the chocolate mixture, salt, vanilla, milk and crumbs.

4. Beat 2 remaining egg whites with an electric mixer on high speed until foamy. Gradually beat in remaining ¼ cup granulated sugar until stiff peaks form when beaters are lifted.

5. Fold beaten whites into chocolate mixture. Scrape into prepared dish. Place dish in baking pan. Pour enough hot water into pan to reach 1 inch up side of dish to make a water bath.

6. Bake 45 minutes, until a thin knife inserted near the center comes out clean. Carefully remove from water bath to a wire rack and let cool until warm.

7. Just before serving, dust with confectioners' sugar. Pass cream to pour over each portion.

Makes 6 servings. Per serving: 551 calories, 8 grams protein, 55 grams carbohydrate, 35 grams fat, 189 milligrams cholesterol with butter, 157 milligrams cholesterol with margarine, 300 milligrams sodium

Mexican Bread Pudding

Monterey Jack cheese is usually used in savory dishes; it's a nice surprise in this pudding.

- 1 cup water
- ½ cup packed brown sugar
- 1 cinnamon stick (about 3 inches long)
- Twelve ½-inch-thick slices bread (4 ounces), cut from a long loaf of Italian or French bread (not sourdough), toasted
- 4 ounces Monterey Jack cheese, cut in ½-inch cubes
- ½ cup raisins
- ¼ cup chopped walnuts, lightly toasted
- ¼ cup slivered almonds, lightly toasted
- ¼ cup pine nuts (pignoli)
- 1 cup heavy cream
- 2 tablespoons granulated sugar
- 1 teaspoon dark rum (optional)
- ½ teaspoon vanilla extract

1. Heat oven to 350°F. Heavily grease an 8-inch square baking pan.

2. Stir water, brown sugar and cinnamon stick in a small heavy saucepan. Bring to a boil over medium-high heat. Boil 5 minutes. Remove from heat. Remove cinnamon stick.

3. Cut bread to fit the bottom of prepared pan in one layer. Sprinkle with cheese, raisins, walnuts, almonds and pine nuts. Pour brown-sugar syrup evenly over all. Cover with foil.

4. Bake 30 minutes. Remove foil and bake 5 minutes longer, until cheese just starts to brown, watching that raisins don't burn. Remove from oven to a wire rack to let cool for a few minutes.

5. Meanwhile, beat cream, granulated sugar, rum, if desired, and vanilla with an electric mixer until soft peaks form when beaters are lifted.

6. Serve pudding hot, topped with cream mixture.

Makes 6 servings. Per serving (with rum): 476 calories, 10 grams protein, 46 grams carbohydrate, 30 grams fat, 72 milligrams cholesterol, 240 milligrams sodium

★ SPECIAL—AND WORTH IT

New Orleans Bread Pudding with Bourbon Sauce

Chunks of bread soaked in milk form the base of a pudding that's topped with an absolutely delicious sauce.

> 1 long loaf (8 ounces) day-old French
>   or Italian bread (not sourdough),
>   cut in ½-inch chunks
> 3 cups milk
> 2 large eggs
> 1 cup granulated sugar
> 1½ tablespoons vanilla extract
> ⅛ teaspoon salt
> ⅔ cup raisins
> 2 tablespoons butter or margarine,
>   melted
> Bourbon Sauce (recipe follows)

1. Heat oven to 350°F. Grease an 8-inch square baking pan.

2. Put bread in a large bowl. Pour in milk and let stand until bread softens. Stir to break up bread slightly. Let stand until almost all the milk is absorbed.

3. Beat eggs, sugar, vanilla and salt in a medium-size bowl until smooth. Stir into bread mixture. Stir in raisins.

4. Scrape into prepared pan. Drizzle butter evenly over top.

5. Bake 1 hour, until a thin knife inserted near the center comes out clean. Remove from oven to a wire rack to let cool to warm.

6. To serve: Cut pudding in rectangles or squares and serve with Bourbon Sauce.

Makes 8 generous servings. Per serving (without sauce): 315 calories, 8 grams protein, 55 grams carbohydrate, 8 grams fat, 70 milligrams cholesterol with butter, 61 milligrams cholesterol with margarine, 300 milligrams sodium

Bourbon Sauce

> ½ cup butter or margarine
> 1 cup granulated sugar
> 1 large egg, lightly beaten
> ½ cup bourbon

1. Melt butter in the top of a double boiler over simmering water. Stir in sugar and egg. Cook, stirring constantly, about 5 minutes, until sauce thickens slightly and registers 160°F on a candy or instant-read thermometer. Remove from heat. Remove top of double boiler. Stir sauce until sugar dissolves.

2. Let sauce cool until warm. Whisk in bourbon. Serve immediately over New Orleans Bread Pudding.

Makes 1½ cups. Per tablespoon: 75 calories, 0 grams protein, 8 grams carbohydrate, 4 grams fat, 19 milligrams cholesterol with butter, 7 milligrams cholesterol with margarine, 49 milligrams sodium

Russian Sharlotka

Pumpernickel bread gives this a subtle flavor—almost like a Christmas pudding. The sour cream enhances the flavor of the wine.

> 6 tablespoons butter or margarine
> 3½ cups fine crumbs from day-old
>   seedless dark pumpernickel
>   bread
> ¾ cup granulated sugar
> ¼ cup dry red wine
> 1 tablespoon lemon juice
> 1½ teaspoons grated fresh orange peel
> ¾ teaspoon ground cinnamon
> ½ teaspoon vanilla extract
> ¼ teaspoon salt
> 5 large tart apples, peeled, cored and
>   very finely chopped (about
>   5 cups)
> ½ cup red-currant jelly
> 1 cup sour cream, stirred smooth

1. Heat oven to 350°F. Grease a 2-quart soufflé dish or round baking dish.

2. Melt butter in a large heavy skillet over medium heat. Add crumbs and cook, stirring constantly, until lightly toasted. Remove from heat.

3. Add sugar, wine, lemon juice, orange peel, cinnamon, vanilla and salt to crumbs and mix well.

4. Sprinkle one fourth of the crumb mixture over bottom of prepared soufflé dish. Top with one third of the apples. Repeat layers twice. Dot with jelly. Sprinkle with remaining crumb mixture.

5. Bake 45 to 50 minutes, until crumbs are well browned and apples are tender when pierced with a fork. Remove from oven to a wire rack to let cool for a few minutes.

6. Serve pudding warm, topped with sour cream.

Makes 8 servings. Per serving: 437 calories, 5 grams protein, 74 grams carbohydrate, 16 grams fat, 40 milligrams cholesterol with butter, 13 milligrams cholesterol with margarine, 355 milligrams sodium

Muffin Pudding
with Maple-Honey Sauce

Serve this pudding hot. It can be made ahead and even frozen. To reheat: Thaw, cover with foil and warm in a preheated 325°F oven for about 30 minutes.

---

  2 **tablespoons butter or margarine, at room temperature**
  1 **cup all-purpose flour**
1¼ **teaspoons ground nutmeg**
 ¼ **teaspoon salt**
  1 **cup milk**
Whites from 2 large eggs, beaten to stiff peaks with an electric mixer
  6 **English muffins, split apart**
 ½ **cup honey**
Maple-Honey Sauce (recipe follows)

1. Have ready a 2-quart steamed-pudding mold, a trivet and a large deep pot with a lid. Put pudding mold on trivet in pot to be sure it fits. Pour enough water into pot to reach halfway up side of mold. Remove mold and grease well with butter. Heat water to a simmer.

2. Meanwhile, put flour, nutmeg and salt in a medium-size bowl and mix well with a fork. Add milk gradually and beat with a fork, a rotary beater or a hand-held electric mixer to make a smooth batter (don't overbeat). Gently fold in beaten egg whites.

3. Loosely fold one muffin half in half, split-side in. Place in bottom of prepared mold fold-side down. Repeat with two more muffin halves.

4. Drizzle a scant tablespoon honey into the fold of each muffin half, then add a large spoonful of the batter. Continue layering muffins, honey and batter, making sure you have enough batter left to cover last layer of muffins.

5. Put lid on mold or cover tightly with a double layer of foil, pressing down muffins if necessary.

6. Place mold on trivet in pot of simmering water. Cover and simmer about 1¼ hours, until a wooden pick inserted in the center of pudding comes out without wet dough sticking to it (damp crumbs means it's done). Remove pudding mold to a wire rack.

7. Remove lid. Let pudding cool in mold on rack 10 minutes. Loosen edges gently with a sharp knife before unmolding onto serving platter. Serve hot with Maple-Honey Sauce.

Makes 8 servings. Per serving (without sauce): 269 calories, 7 grams protein, 39 grams carbohydrate, 5 grams fat, 15 milligrams cholesterol with butter, 6 milligrams cholesterol with margarine, 319 milligrams sodium

Maple-Honey Sauce

 ½ **cup pure maple syrup**
 ¼ **cup honey**
 ¼ **cup butter or margarine**

1. Put maple syrup, honey and butter in a small saucepan. Place over medium heat and cook, stirring constantly, until butter melts and sauce is smooth and hot.

2. Serve hot over Muffin Pudding.

Makes about 1 cup. Per 2 tablespoons: 133 calories, 0 grams protein, 22 grams carbohydrate, 6 grams fat, 18 milligrams cholesterol with butter, 0 milligrams cholesterol with margarine, 71 milligrams sodium

Muffin Pudding with Maple-Honey Sauce, Fresh Orange-Cranberry Compote

Jeweled Bread Pudding

The idea for this recipe came from Trader Vic, owner of the former New York City restaurant that was famous for exotic drinks. Trader Vic's mother served her version with quince jelly and whipped cream.

- 2 large eggs
- ½ cup granulated sugar
- 2 tablespoons butter or margarine, melted
- 2¼ cups milk
- 1 teaspoon vanilla extract
- ½ teaspoon ground cinnamon
- ¼ teaspoon ground nutmeg
- ¼ teaspoon salt
- 2 cups ½-inch cubes day-old French or Italian bread (not sourdough) or firm white bread (homemade is best)
- ⅓ cup raisins
- 5 tablespoons quince or tart apple jelly, at room temperature
- ½ cup heavy cream, whipped to soft peaks

1. Heat oven to 350°F. Grease a shallow 1½-quart baking dish. Have a shallow baking pan ready.

2. Beat eggs lightly in a medium-size bowl. Beat in sugar and butter, then milk, vanilla, cinnamon, nutmeg and salt. Stir in bread and raisins.

3. Pour mixture into prepared baking dish. Place baking dish in baking pan. Pour enough hot water into pan to reach 1 inch up side of dish to make a water bath.

4. Bake 55 minutes, until a thin knife inserted near the center comes out clean. Remove from water bath to a wire rack. Let cool until warm.

5. Spoon pudding onto dessert plates and top each serving with a spoonful of jelly and a dollop of whipped cream.

Makes 6 servings. Per serving: 347 calories, 7 grams protein, 44 grams carbohydrate, 17 grams fat, 116 milligrams cholesterol with butter, 104 milligrams cholesterol with margarine, 262 milligrams sodium

Brown-Sugar Casserole Pudding

When unmolded, this pudding forms its own rich sauce.

- ¾ cup packed dark-brown sugar
- 3 slices day-old firm white bread
- 2 tablespoons butter or margarine, at room temperature
- 1 cup raisins
- 3 large eggs
- 2 cups milk
- 1 tablespoon dark rum
- 1 teaspoon vanilla extract
- ¼ teaspoon salt
- Heavy cream

1. Heat oven to 350°F. Sprinkle sugar over the bottom of a deep 1½-quart casserole. Have a shallow baking pan ready.

2. Spread both sides of the bread with butter; cut in ½-inch cubes. Arrange in sugared casserole. Sprinkle bread cubes with raisins.

3. Beat eggs lightly in a medium-size bowl. Beat in milk, rum, vanilla and salt. Pour mixture over raisins.

4. Place casserole in baking pan. Pour enough hot water into pan to reach 1 inch up side of casserole to make a water bath.

5. Bake 50 to 60 minutes, until a thin knife inserted near the center comes out clean. Remove from water bath to a wire rack. Let pudding stand about 10 minutes.

6. To unmold: Loosen pudding around edges with a thin knife. Invert onto a high-sided platter to catch the sauce.

7. Spoon pudding into dessert bowls. Serve hot with cream.

Makes 6 servings. Per serving (without cream): 332 calories, 8 grams protein, 55 grams carbohydrate, 10 grams fat, 119 milligrams cholesterol with butter, 107 milligrams cholesterol with margarine, 279 milligrams sodium

Golden Pudding

This lovely old recipe is made entirely on top of the range.

⅓ cup granulated sugar
1½ cups water
1 cinnamon stick (about 3 inches long)
⅓ cup ground or finely grated blanched almonds
Yolks from 4 large eggs
3 tablespoons unsalted butter or margarine
1½ cups ½-inch cubes day-old French or Italian bread (not sourdough)

1. Mix sugar, water and cinnamon stick in a heavy saucepan (not uncoated aluminum). Bring to a boil over high heat. Boil 3 minutes without stirring. Stir in almonds. Remove from heat. Stir briefly to let cool slightly.

2. Beat egg yolks with an electric mixer on high speed about 5 minutes, until slightly thickened and pale.

3. Continue beating yolks while gradually pouring in hot almond syrup until well blended. Return mixture to saucepan.

4. Place egg mixture over low heat and cook about 5 minutes, stirring constantly, until mixture thickens slightly, coats a metal spoon and registers 160°F on a candy or instant-read thermometer. Remove from heat. Discard cinnamon stick.

5. Scrape mixture into a shallow serving dish.

6. Melt butter in a medium-size heavy skillet over medium heat. Add bread cubes and cook about 5 minutes, stirring constantly, until very crisp and deep golden brown.

7. Sprinkle bread cubes over egg mixture. Serve warm.

Makes 4 servings. Per serving: 295 calories, 6 grams protein, 24 grams carbohydrate, 20 grams fat, 215 milligrams cholesterol with butter, 188 milligrams cholesterol with margarine, 66 milligrams sodium

🕐 **MAKE-AHEAD**
Mother's Cup Puddings

A tender custard with raisins, just like the one Mom or Dad used to make when you needed comforting.

2 slices day-old firm white bread (homemade is best), cut in ½-inch cubes
⅓ cup raisins
3 large eggs
½ cup granulated sugar
2 cups milk
1½ teaspoons vanilla extract
½ teaspoon salt
⅛ teaspoon ground cinnamon
Ground nutmeg
Heavy cream

1. Heat oven to 350°F. Grease six 6-ounce custard cups. Have a shallow baking pan ready.

2. Divide bread among custard cups. Sprinkle with raisins.

3. Beat eggs lightly in a medium-size bowl. Beat in sugar, then milk, vanilla, salt and cinnamon.

4. Pour milk mixture into custard cups. Sprinkle with nutmeg.

5. Place custard cups in baking pan. Pour enough hot water into pan to reach ½ inch up sides of cups to make a water bath.

6. Bake 40 minutes, until a thin knife inserted near centers of custards comes out clean. Remove from water bath to a wire rack. Let cool until warm and serve or chill.

7. Serve custards with heavy cream.

Makes 6 servings. Per serving (without cream): 202 calories, 7 grams protein, 31 grams carbohydrate, 6 grams fat, 107 milligrams cholesterol, 289 milligrams sodium

---

Pudding Safety Tips

Use the following tips to keep puddings and custards safe and wholesome.

☐ Let egg-rich puddings and custards cool on a wire rack only until warm, not lukewarm or room temperature. Then serve immediately or cover partially (vent one end of plastic wrap or foil) and refrigerate.

☐ Refrigerate all leftovers as soon as possible.

☐ Allow plenty of air circulation around the dessert in the refrigerator.

Chilled Bread Pudding

Good served with a fruit sauce such as Double Blueberry Sauce (page 114) or Strawberry-Patch Sauce (page 118).

1½ cups soft fresh whole-wheat
    bread crumbs
1 cup packed brown sugar
¼ teaspoon salt
2 envelopes unflavored gelatin
½ cup cold water
3 cups heavy cream
⅓ cup granulated sugar
¼ teaspoon vanilla extract

1. Heat oven to 450°F. Line a 13x9-inch baking pan with foil. Have ready a 1-quart soufflé dish fitted with a 3-inch foil collar (see Making a Soufflé Collar, page 85).

2. Mix bread crumbs, brown sugar and salt with fingers in prepared pan until crumbly. Spread evenly in pan. Bake about 12 minutes, stirring occasionally, until the sugar caramelizes. Remove from oven and let cool on a wire rack.

3. Finely crush cooled crumbs with a rolling pin or in a food processor.

4. Sprinkle gelatin over cold water in a small saucepan and let soften 1 minute. Stir over low heat until gelatin is dissolved. Remove from heat and let cool to lukewarm.

5. Pour gelatin mixture into electric-mixer bowl. Add heavy cream, granulated sugar and vanilla. Beat on medium-high speed until stiff peaks form when beaters are lifted. Fold in crumb mixture with a large rubber spatula.

6. Scrape mixture into prepared soufflé dish. Gently smooth the top with spatula. Chill at least 2 hours, until pudding is set. Remove foil collar and serve.

Makes 8 servings. Per serving: 477 calories, 4 grams protein, 42 grams carbohydrate, 34 grams fat, 119 milligrams cholesterol, 154 milligrams sodium

Woman's Day Special Matzo-Apple Pudding

A great Passover dessert or—with half the sugar—a good side dish.

3 whole square matzos, broken up
6 large eggs
3 medium-size apples, peeled, cored
    and chopped
¾ cup raisins
¾ cup packed brown sugar
¼ cup margarine, melted
2 teaspoons ground cinnamon
¼ teaspoon ground nutmeg
¼ teaspoon salt

1. Heat oven to 350°F. Grease a deep 2-quart casserole.

2. Put matzos in a medium-size bowl and add water to cover. Soak matzos until soft. Drain off water. Squeeze matzos dry and set aside on a plate. Dry the bowl.

3. Lightly beat eggs in same bowl. Add matzos, apples, raisins, brown sugar, margarine, cinnamon, nutmeg and salt and mix well.

4. Pour mixture into prepared casserole. Bake 45 to 50 minutes, until pudding is firm and top is lightly browned. Remove from oven to a wire rack to let cool for a few minutes.

5. Serve warm.

Makes 10 servings. Per serving: 235 calories, 4 grams protein, 36 grams carbohydrate, 8 grams fat, 116 milligrams cholesterol, 154 milligrams sodium

Trifles

🕐 **MAKE-AHEAD**
★ **SPECIAL—AND WORTH IT**
✳ **MICROWAVE**

English Trifle

This dessert is great for entertaining, since you refrigerate it overnight before serving.

Yolks from 3 large eggs
  3 **tablespoons granulated sugar**
  1 **cup milk**
  1 **cup heavy cream**
  2 **tablespoons confectioners' sugar**
  1 **package (3 ounces) unfilled ladyfingers**
  6 **tablespoons seedless red-raspberry jam**
12 **amaretti cookies or 12 vanilla**
      wafers, crushed (about 1 cup)
  2 **tablespoons toasted slivered almonds**
⅓ **cup dry sherry wine or orange juice**

1. Have ready a 1- to 1½-quart serving bowl (preferably glass).

2. Whisk egg yolks and granulated sugar in a small bowl until thickened and pale.

3. Heat milk in a small heavy saucepan over low heat just until small bubbles form around the edges. Gradually whisk into yolk mixture. Pour mixture into a clean small heavy saucepan. Stir over low heat 3 to 4 minutes, until custard is slightly thickened, coats a metal spoon and registers 160°F on a candy or instant-read thermometer.

4. Immediately set saucepan in a bowl of ice water and stir mixture occasionally until cool.

5. With an electric mixer on high speed, whip cream with confectioners' sugar until stiff peaks form when beaters are lifted.

6. To assemble trifle: Spread flat sides of one strip of ladyfingers with 3 tablespooons of the jam and top with remaining strip flat-side down. Cut ladyfingers apart. Arrange over bottom and around sides of bowl, cutting ladyfingers in half if necessary. Sprinkle cookie crumbs, then almonds over ladyfingers in bottom of bowl. Drizzle with sherry and spoon on custard. Spread whipped cream over top.

7. Cover trifle and refrigerate overnight.

8. To garnish: Stir remaining 3 tablespoons jam until smooth and runny. Drop by small spoonfuls on whipped cream. Using tip of a knife, "pull" jam through cream for a marbleized effect. Serve immediately.

Makes 8 servings. Per serving (with sherry): 285 calories, 4 grams protein, 27 grams carbohydrate, 17 grams fat, 153 milligrams cholesterol, 38 milligrams sodium

Microwave Method: Mix sugar and 1 tablespoon cornstarch in a 4-cup microwave-safe glass measure. Whisk in milk. Microwave on high 4 to 5 minutes, until boiling and thickened. Whisk egg yolks in a small bowl. Stir in a small amount of milk mixture, then whisk yolk mixture into remaining milk mixture until blended. Microwave on high 30 seconds, until mixture registers 160°F on a candy or instant-read thermometer. Let cool to warm; cover and chill. (Custard thickens as it chills.) Proceed as directed.

🕐 **MAKE-AHEAD**

Quick Strawberry Trifles

  1 **quart basket strawberries (about 6 cups)**
  3 **tablespoons granulated sugar, or to taste**
  2 **tablespoons water**
  1 **container (8 ounces) frozen**
      nondairy whipped topping, thawed
12 **unfilled lady fingers**

1. Reserve 6 pretty berries for garnish. Rinse and hull the remaining berries.

2. Process about half the berries with the sugar and water in a food processor or blender until almost puréed but still chunky. Scrape into a large bowl.

3. Thinly slice the remaining berries (except the berries reserved for garnish). Stir sliced berries into the purée. Fold in the whipped topping.

4. Spoon the mixture into 6 dessert bowls. Cut the lady fingers in half crosswise. Stick cut-ends down into the strawberry cream around the edge of each bowl. Garnish with the reserved berries and serve, or chill up to 1 hour before serving.

Makes 6 servings: Per serving. 254 calories, 3 grams protein, 36 grams carbohydrate, 12 grams fat, 78 milligrams cholesterol, 26 milligrams sodium

---

Trifles

Elizabeth Alston, the British-born food editor of *Woman's Day*, offers the following recommendations for a fabulous trifle: "First, start with good cake, ladyfingers, pound cake or champagne biscuits. You need a lavish hand with the sherry (a delicious variation would be fresh orange juice or orange-flavor liqueur). Next pour on a good egg-rich custard and top with plenty of real whipped cream. When this sort of trifle is for dessert, you might as well skip the main course."

Raspberry-Vanilla Trifle

Thaw raspberries in a bowl to collect the juices. This trifle is best when made a day ahead.

---

1 package (4-serving size) vanilla pudding and pie filling (not instant pudding)
2¾ cups milk
2 packages (10 ounces each) frozen raspberries in syrup, thawed
¾ cup dry sherry wine or orange juice
1 pound cake (about 10¾ ounces), thawed if frozen

For garnish: ½ cup heavy cream

1. Cook pudding according to package directions, using the milk. Scrape into a medium-size bowl.

2. Cover pudding with waxed paper or plastic wrap to prevent skin from forming. Refrigerate 3 hours, until cold, or overnight.

3. To assemble trifle: Have ready a wide 2- to 2½-quart serving bowl (preferably glass).

4. Drain raspberries thoroughly in a strainer suspended over a medium-size bowl or a large glass measure. Measure out ¾ cup drained raspberry liquid and mix with sherry.

5. Slice cake crosswise in 10 pieces. Arrange 5 slices in the bottom of serving bowl, cutting cake to fit if necessary. Pour half the sherry mixture over cake. Top with half the raspberries, then half the pudding. Repeat layers. Cover and refrigerate at least 4 hours or overnight.

6. To serve: Beat cream with an electric mixer on high speed until stiff peaks form when beaters are lifted. Pipe or spoon cream on trifle and serve.

Makes 8 servings. Per serving (with sherry, without cream): 370 calories, 6 grams protein, 51 grams carbohydrate, 14 grams fat, 67 milligrams cholesterol, 132 milligrams sodium

Chocolate-Apricot Trifle

This company-special dessert can be prepared a day ahead. Use a serrated knife to split the cake in layers.

½ cup unsweetened cocoa powder
½ cup plus 2 tablespoons granulated sugar
2 teaspoons cornstarch
¼ teaspoon salt
2½ cups milk or half-and-half
1 large egg
1 teaspoon vanilla extract
1 cup apricot preserves (12 ounces)
¼ cup brandy or orange juice
1 cup heavy cream
1 angel-food cake, homemade or purchased, split in 4 layers
¼ cup slivered or sliced almonds, toasted

1. Mix cocoa, ½ cup of the sugar, the cornstarch and salt in a medium-size heavy saucepan. Stir in milk until blended. Stir over medium heat until mixture comes to a full boil and is smooth and thickened. Remove from heat.

2. Lightly beat egg in a small bowl. Stir a small amount of the hot mixture into the egg, then stir into chocolate sauce.

3. Stir sauce over very low heat 1 to 2 minutes, until it is slightly thickened, coats a metal spoon and registers 160°F on a candy or instant-read thermometer (do not boil). Remove from heat; stir in vanilla.

4. Let sauce cool until warm, stirring occasionally. Transfer to a medium-size bowl. Cover and chill.

5. Mix preserves and brandy in a small bowl until well blended.

6. Beat cream and remaining 2 tablespoons sugar with an electric mixer on high speed until stiff peaks form when beaters are lifted.

7. To assemble trifle: Place one cake layer in a shallow serving bowl with a flat bottom. Spread cake with one third of the apricot mixture, then with one third of the whipped cream. Repeat process with two more cake layers. Top with fourth cake layer.

8. Cover and chill at least 2 hours or overnight.

9. Drizzle chilled chocolate sauce over the trifle. Sprinkle with almonds. Serve immediately.

Makes 8 servings. Per serving (with milk and brandy): 602 calories, 10 grams protein, 101 grams carbohydrate, 18 grams fat, 78 milligrams cholesterol, 246 milligrams sodium

Raspberry-Vanilla Trifle

Sherry-Fruit Trifle

Assemble this dessert in a glass bowl to show off the multicolored layers. Make and refrigerate at least four hours or up to one day in advance.

- 1 package (3 ounces) unfilled ladyfingers
- 3 tablespoons seedless raspberry or strawberry jam
- ¼ cup cream sherry wine (optional)
- 1 can (about 16 ounces) fruit cocktail in juice, drained and juice reserved
- ½ cup firmly set raspberry or strawberry gelatin (see Note), cut in small pieces
- 2 to 3 tablespoons milk
- 1 package (3½ ounces) instant vanilla pudding and pie-filling mix, prepared according to package directions

For garnish: whipped cream and additional gelatin pieces

1. Tear ladyfingers in bite-size pieces and arrange in bottom of a 1½-quart bowl or soufflé dish.

2. Stir jam until smooth and drizzle over ladyfingers. Sprinkle with sherry and drizzle with a few teaspoons of the reserved fruit-cocktail juice. If not using sherry, increase amount of fruit-cocktail juice to ¼ cup.

3. Spoon fruit cocktail over ladyfingers in an even layer. Scatter gelatin pieces on top.

4. Stir milk into prepared pudding until it's the consistency of a thin custard sauce. Pour over top of trifle.

5. Cover with plastic wrap and refrigerate at least 4 hours or up to 1 day.

6. Just before serving, garnish with whipped cream and scatter additional gelatin pieces over cream.

Makes 8 servings. Per serving (with sherry): 178 calories, 3 grams protein, 35 grams carbohydrate, 3 grams fat, 47 milligrams cholesterol, 240 milligrams sodium

Note: Prepare a 4-serving-size package of gelatin according to package directions. Chill until firm. Scoop out ½ cup of the gelatin for the trifle. Use the rest for the garnish and for dessert another day.

Zuppa Inglese

The Italian version of the English trifle.

- ½ cup seedless raspberry jam
- ¼ cup light rum
- 1 package (10 ounces, 2 layers) sponge cake, each layer split horizontally
- 1 recipe Basic Stirred Custard (recipe, page 60), chilled
- ½ cup heavy cream
- 1 tablespoon granulated sugar

1. Measure and set aside 3 tablespoons of the jam. Stir remaining jam with the rum in a small bowl until smooth and well blended.

2. Place one cake layer in a shallow serving dish. Spread with one third of the raspberry mixture. Spoon on about one fourth of the custard, letting it run over the sides. Repeat procedure with two more cake layers. Top with fourth layer. Drizzle remaining custard over cake.

3. Whip cream and sugar with an electric mixer on high speed until stiff peaks form when beaters are lifted.

4. Decorate top of cake with dollops of whipped cream and reserved raspberry jam. Chill at least 1 hour before cutting in wedges and serving.

Makes 8 servings. Per serving: 324 calories, 7 grams protein, 45 grams carbohydrate, 11 grams fat, 196 milligrams cholesterol, 155 milligrams sodium

Mousses

♥ LOW-CALORIE

Slim Chocolate Mousse
(Shown on page 64)

Yes, you can make a great mousse without eggs, heavy cream or high-fat chocolate.

½ cup canned evaporated low-fat
   (2%-fat) milk
1½ teaspoons unflavored gelatin
6 tablespoons water
¼ cup unsweetened cocoa powder
⅓ cup granulated sugar
1 teaspoon vanilla extract

1. Put evaporated milk in a small bowl and freeze about 30 minutes, until ice crystals begin to form around edges.

2. Sprinkle gelatin over 2 tablespoons of the water in a cup. Let stand 1 minute to soften.

3. Meanwhile, put remaining 4 tablespoons water, the cocoa powder and sugar in a small heavy saucepan. Cook over medium-low heat 2 to 3 minutes, stirring occasionally, until sugar has dissolved. Reduce heat to low, add gelatin mixture and stir until gelatin is completely dissolved. Remove from heat.

4. Pour cocoa mixture into a large bowl and let cool to room temperature.

5. Meanwhile, remove milk from freezer, add vanilla and beat with an electric mixer on medium-high speed until stiff peaks form.

6. Stir a spoonful of the beaten milk into the cocoa mixture until blended, then gently fold in the remaining beaten milk.

7. Spoon into six dessert glasses and chill 1 hour, until set. Serve.

Makes 6 servings, ⅔ cup each. Per serving: 74 calories, 3 grams protein, 15 grams carbohydrate, 1 gram fat, 3 milligrams cholesterol, 23 milligrams sodium

🕐 MAKE-AHEAD
Chocolate-Mint Mousse

A light refreshing mousse. The recipe is easily doubled.

3 squares (1 ounce each) semisweet
   chocolate, broken up
2 tablespoons crème de menthe
2 tablespoons water
⅓ cup thawed frozen cholesterol-free
   egg product
1 tablespoon meringue powder and
   ¼ cup cup cold water, or whites
   from 2 large eggs (see Egg Safety,
   page 57)
¼ cup sugar
½ cup heavy cream

1. Mix chocolate, crème de menthe and water in a medium-size heavy saucepan. Cook over low heat, stirring occasionally, until chocolate is melted and mixture is smooth. Remove from heat. Let cool 5 minutes.

2. Beat egg product in a medium-size bowl with a wire whisk until frothy. Slowly beat warm chocolate mixture into egg product just until smooth.

3. Beat meringue powder and cold water (or egg whites) with an electric mixer on high speed until soft peaks form when beaters are lifted. Gradually beat in sugar until mixture is stiff but not dry.

4. Gently fold one fourth of the beaten meringue powder into chocolate mixture, then gently fold chocolate mixture into remaining meringue.

5. With same beaters, beat cream until soft peaks form when beaters are lifted.

6. Fold whipped cream into chocolate mixture until blended.

7. Spoon mousse into four dessert bowls or wine glasses. Cover and chill several hours before serving.

Makes 4 servings. Per serving (with meringue powder): 294 calories, 5 grams protein, 30 grams carbohydrate, 17 grams fat, 33 milligrams cholesterol, 74 grams sodium

(See overleaf) Peach Mousse, Melba Sauce, Cold Lemon Soufflé and Strawberry Mousse

Peach Mousse with Melba Sauce

(Shown on page 78)

If you don't want to mold this dessert, pour it into a bowl, a collared 1-quart soufflé dish (see Making a Soufflé Collar, page 85) or elegant wine goblets.

---

 3 envelopes unflavored gelatin
 ¾ cup cold water
 2 pounds fresh ripe peaches (about
     7 medium-size), peeled (see
     Peaches, page 24), halved, pitted
     and cut in small chunks
 ¼ cup peach preserves
 ¼ cup granulated sugar
 2 tablespoons lemon juice
 ¾ cup plain low-fat yogurt
 2 tablespoons peach-flavor brandy,
     peach nectar or water
 1½ cups part-skim ricotta cheese
For garnish: sliced peaches, fresh
     raspberries and mint leaves
Melba Sauce (recipe follows)

1. Have a 6-cup ring mold ready.

2. Sprinkle gelatin over water in a 3-quart bowl. Let stand 1 minute to soften.

3. Meanwhile, purée peaches, in batches if necessary, in a food processor or a blender (you should have 4 cups purée). Scrape purée into a medium-size saucepan (not uncoated aluminum).

4. Add preserves, sugar and lemon juice to peach purée. Bring to a boil over medium-high heat. Cook about 2 minutes, stirring constantly, until preserves and sugar dissolve. Remove from heat.

5. Pour hot purée over softened gelatin and stir 3 minutes, until gelatin dissolves completely. Stir in yogurt and brandy until well blended.

6. Cover and refrigerate about 1 hour, stirring three times, until mixture thickens to the consistency of unbeaten egg whites and mounds slightly when dropped from a spoon.

7. Process ricotta in a food processor or a blender until smooth and creamy. Fold into peach mixture.

8. Lightly oil ring mold and gently pour in mousse mixture. Cover loosely and refrigerate at least 3 hours, until mousse is completely set.

9. To unmold: Dip mold up to the rim in warm, not hot, water for about 5 seconds. Run tip of a thin knife around the edge of mold and center tube. Invert serving plate over mold and, holding both tightly together, turn both over. Lift off mold.

10. Fill center of mousse with sliced peaches, raspberries and mint leaves in a decorative manner. Cut into portions and serve with Melba Sauce on the side.

Makes 8 servings. Per serving (with brandy, without garnish or sauce): 181 calories, 9 grams protein, 28 grams carbohydrate, 4 grams fat, 16 milligrams cholesterol, 73 milligrams sodium

Melba Sauce

 1 cup (6 ounces) fresh or frozen
     unsweetened raspberries
 ¼ cup raspberry preserves
 3 tablespoons granulated sugar
 1 tablespoon lemon juice
 1 tablespoon raspberry-flavor liqueur
     (optional)

1. Mix raspberries, preserves, sugar and lemon juice in a small saucepan (not uncoated aluminum). Bring to a boil over medium-high heat. Reduce heat to low and simmer 5 to 7 minutes, stirring occasionally, until berries release their juices and soften. Remove from heat.

2. Press raspberry mixture through a fine strainer suspended over a small bowl. Discard seeds. Let mixture cool to room temperature. Stir in liqueur, if desired.

3. Cover and chill until ready to serve.

Makes ⅔ cup. Per tablespoon (with liqueur): 40 calories, 0 grams protein, 10 grams carbohydrate, 0 grams fat, 0 milligrams cholesterol, 1 milligram sodium

Strawberry Mousse

(Shown on page 79)

The success of this dessert depends on the berries, which should be very ripe and full of flavor. You can spoon this mousse into wine glasses instead of serving it from a bowl.

> 5 cups ripe strawberries, rinsed, drained, and hulled; save 8 pretty berries for garnish
> 3 envelopes unflavored gelatin
> ¾ cup cold water
> ¼ cup strawberry jelly
> ¼ cup granulated sugar
> 1 cup plain low-fat yogurt
> 1¼ cups part-skim ricotta cheese

1. Purée strawberries in a food processor, in a blender or with a food mill. Press through a fine strainer suspended over a large bowl to remove seeds; discard seeds (you should have 3 cups purée).

2. Sprinkle gelatin over water in a small saucepan. Let stand 1 minute to soften. Place over low heat 3 to 5 minutes, stirring constantly, until liquid is almost boiling and gelatin is completely dissolved. Add jelly and sugar to gelatin and stir just until dissolved. Remove from heat.

3. Stir gelatin mixture into strawberry purée. Stir in yogurt.

4. Cover and refrigerate about 1 hour, stirring three times, until mixture thickens to the consistency of unbeaten egg whites and mounds slightly when dropped from a spoon.

5. Process ricotta in a food processor or a blender until smooth and creamy. Fold into strawberry mixture and pour into a 1½-quart serving bowl.

6. Cover loosely and refrigerate at least 3 hours, until mousse is completely set.

7. Garnish with reserved berries and serve.

Makes 8 servings. Per serving: 160 calories, 8 grams protein, 24 grams carbohydrate, 4 grams fat, 14 milligrams cholesterol, 67 milligrams sodium

Summer-Fruit Mousse

🕐 **MAKE-AHEAD**

Summer-Fruit Mousse

The fruit purée can be made up to a day ahead and refrigerated, but don't make the mousse more than two hours before serving. This recipe can be adapted to use most summer fruits and berries. Adjust the amounts of sugar and lemon juice to the fruit.

> 1 pint basket ripe strawberries, rinsed, drained, hulled and halved (about 3 cups)
> ¼ cup plus 1½ tablespoons granulated sugar
> 2 teaspoons fresh-squeezed lemon juice
> ⅛ teaspoon salt
> 1 teaspoon grated fresh orange peel
> 1 cup heavy cream
> ½ teaspoon vanilla extract

1. Beat strawberries, ¼ cup of the sugar, the lemon juice and salt with electric mixer on medium speed until almost smooth. Stir in orange peel. Measure out and reserve ⅓ cup for garnish.

2. With clean beaters in a clean bowl, beat cream, remaining 1½ tablespoons sugar and the vanilla on high speed until soft peaks form when beaters are lifted. Fold in remaining purée until blended.

3. Spoon about ½ cup cream mixture into each of six wine glasses or dessert bowls. Cover with plastic wrap and refrigerate up to 2 hours.

4. To serve: Top each glass with a spoonful of reserved fruit purée.

Makes 6 servings. Per serving: 200 calories, 1 gram protein, 16 grams carbohydrate, 15 grams fat, 53 milligrams cholesterol, 59 milligrams sodium

Plum, Anise and Yogurt Mousse

3. Add gelatin to plum mixture and stir over low heat 1 to 2 minutes, until gelatin is completely dissolved.

4. Purée plum mixture in a food processor or a blender until fairly smooth (you should have 2 cups).

5. Pour purée into a medium-size bowl. Refrigerate about 1 hour, stirring three times, until mixture thickens to the consistency of unbeaten egg whites and mounds slightly when dropped from a spoon.

6. Meanwhile, put evaporated milk in a small bowl and place in freezer about 30 minutes, until it begins to freeze around the edges. Beat with an electric mixer on medium-high speed until foamy. Add remaining 1 tablespoon sugar and continue beating until stiff peaks form when beaters are lifted.

7. Stir yogurt until smooth, then stir into plum mixture.

8. Fold beaten milk into plum mixture.

9. Spoon into six stemmed dessert glasses. Cover and chill at least 4 hours, until set, or overnight. Serve.

Makes 5 cups; 6 servings. Per serving: 98 calories, 5 grams protein, 21 grams carbohydrate, 0 grams fat, 2 milligrams cholesterol, 54 milligrams sodium

---

○ **MAKE-AHEAD**
♥ **LOW-CALORIE**

Plum, Anise and Yogurt Mousse

The anise adds a delicate licorice flavor.

12 **ounces very ripe plums, halved, pitted and thinly sliced (about 2 cups)**
⅔ **cup unsweetened white grape juice**
2 **tablespoons granulated sugar**
¼ **teaspoon anise seed, finely chopped**
1 **envelope unflavored gelatin**
½ **cup evaporated skimmed milk**
1 **cup plain nonfat yogurt**

1. Put plums, ⅓ cup of the grape juice, 1 tablespoon of the sugar and the anise seed in a medium-size saucepan (not uncoated aluminum). Bring to a boil over medium-high heat. Reduce heat to medium-low and simmer 8 to 10 minutes, until plums are very tender and juices have thickened and are syrupy. Remove from heat.

2. Sprinkle gelatin over remaining ⅓ cup grape juice. Let stand 1 minute to soften.

○ **MAKE-AHEAD**

Brandied White Chocolate Mousse

12 **ounces white chocolate**
2 **cups heavy cream**
3 **tablespoons confectioners' sugar**
2 **tablespoons brandy or rum**

1. Melt chocolate with ⅔ cup of the cream in a medium-size heavy saucepan over low heat or in the top of a double boiler over barely simmering water, stirring, until mixture is smooth. Remove from heat and let cool to room temperature.

2. Whip remaining 1⅓ cups cream with the sugar and brandy until almost-stiff peaks form when beaters are lifted.

3. Fold a small amount of whipped cream into cooled chocolate. Pour chocolate over cream and fold until smooth.

4. Spoon into eight or ten wine glasses or coffee cups. Chill at least 1 hour before serving.

Makes 8 to 10 servings. Per serving (one tenth): 364 calories, 3 grams protein, 25 grams carbohydrate, 28 grams fat, 71 milligrams cholesterol, 46 milligrams sodium

Mascarpone Brandy Mousse

Mascarpone—a rich, fresh dessert cheese—is available in shops carrying Italian specialties and in fancy food shops. You can substitute cream cheese with very good results. This dessert can be made up to 24 hours ahead.

½ cup thawed frozen cholesterol-free
    egg product
½ cup plus 2 tablespoons granulated
    sugar
1½ teaspoons brandy or 1 teaspoon
    vanilla extract
8 ounces very fresh mascarpone or
    cream cheese, at room
    temperature
Pinch of salt if using cream cheese
1 tablespoon meringue powder and
    ¼ cup cold water (see Egg Safety,
    page 57), or whites from 2 large
    eggs
For garnish: 1 tablespoon shaved or
    grated unsweetened chocolate

1. Beat egg product in a medium-size bowl with a wire whisk just until foamy. Whisk in ½ cup of the sugar until dissolved. Whisk in brandy.

2. Beat mascarpone (or cream cheese and salt) with an electric mixer on medium-high speed until smooth and fluffy.

3. Gradually beat egg mixture into cheese and beat on medium-high speed 2 to 3 minutes, until well blended and smooth.

4. In a clean bowl with clean beaters, beat meringue powder and water (or the egg whites) on high speed until foamy. Gradually beat in remaining 2 tablespoons sugar. Continue beating until soft peaks form when beaters are lifted.

5. Gently fold beaten meringue powder into cheese mixture until thoroughly combined.

6. Spoon about ⅓ cup into each of eight small wine glasses. Sprinkle with chocolate.

7. Cover loosely and refrigerate until ready to serve.

Makes 3½ cups; 8 servings. Per serving (made with cream cheese and salt, brandy and meringue powder): 74 calories, 5 grams protein, 17 grams carbohydrate, 10 grams fat, 31 milligrams cholesterol, 141 milligrams sodium

Brandy-Alexander Mousse

(Shown on page 46)

This dense velvety mousse is very easy to make.

3 squares (1 ounce each) semisweet
    chocolate, broken up
1 cup heavy cream
¼ cup granulated sugar
⅛ teaspoon salt
⅓ cup thawed frozen cholesterol-free
    egg product
2 tablespoons brandy or 2 teaspoons
    vanilla extract

1. Heat chocolate, ½ cup of the cream, the sugar and salt in a small saucepan over low heat, stirring occasionally, until chocolate melts and mixture is smooth. Remove from heat.

2. Put egg product in a food processor or a blender and process 20 seconds, until foamy. With machine on, add warm chocolate mixture in a slow steady stream. Or whisk egg product in a medium-size bowl, then gradually add warm chocolate mixture in a slow steady stream, whisking constantly.

3. Scrape mixture into a medium-size bowl and stir in brandy until smooth. Partially cover with plastic wrap and refrigerate until no longer warm.

4. Beat remaining ½ cup cream with an electric mixer on high speed until soft peaks form when beaters are lifted. Fold cream gently into chocolate mixture.

5. Pour into four demitasse cups or small cordial glasses. Cover and chill at least 1 hour before serving.

Makes 4 servings. Per serving (with brandy): 360 calories, 4 grams protein, 27 grams carbohydrate, 26 grams fat, 66 milligrams cholesterol, 125 milligrams sodium

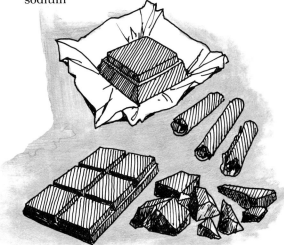

Soufflés

Apricot Mini-Soufflés

This light-as-air dessert is a breeze to prepare. It may sound rather unusual to use baby food in an adult recipe, but it works beautifully and eliminates the need to purée apricots.

2 tablespoons butter or margarine, at
  room temperature
⅔ cup granulated sugar
1 jar (7½ ounces) junior apricots
  with tapioca
4 large eggs, separated
½ teaspoon grated fresh lemon peel
Pinch of salt
Confectioners' sugar (optional)

1. Heat oven to 400°F. Have a baking sheet ready. Generously grease five 6-ounce ramekins or custard cups with butter. Divide ⅓ cup of the granulated sugar among ramekins. Turn ramekins to coat sides and bottoms evenly.

2. Mix remaining ⅓ cup granulated sugar, the apricots, egg yolks and lemon peel in a large bowl.

3. Beat egg whites and salt with an electric mixer on high speed until stiff peaks form when beaters are lifted.

4. Stir one third of the beaten whites into the yolk mixture to lighten it. Gently fold in the remaining whites with a rubber spatula.

5. Gently spoon apricot mixture into the ramekins. Arrange ramekins on baking sheet for easier handling.

6. Bake 12 minutes, until soufflés have risen and tops are golden. Remove from oven.

7. Dust tops with confectioners' sugar, if desired, and serve immediately.

Makes 5 servings. Per serving (without confectioners' sugar): 240 calories, 5 grams protein, 27 grams carbohydrate, 9 grams fat, 168 milligrams cholesterol with butter, 164 milligrams cholesterol with margarine, 131 milligrams sodium

Apricot Mini Soufflés

Making a Soufflé Collar

☐ A collar supports a hot soufflé as it rises; it's used in a cold soufflé to give that illusion. Use a straight-sided soufflé dish or a ramekin, grease it well and fit it with a collar.

☐ Tear off a length of waxed paper or foil about 2 to 3 inches longer than needed to wrap around a soufflé dish or a ramekin. For a 1- to 1½-quart soufflé dish, fold the paper or foil in half lengthwise. For ramekins, cut the paper in half lengthwise, then fold each strip in half lengthwise (you'll have enough for two ramekins).

☐ Lightly oil one side (only if making a cold soufflé; otherwise grease collar when greasing dish) and wrap around dish oiled side in, using a paper clip, a pin or string to fasten to outside of dish.

☐ When the soufflé is ready to serve, run the blade of a thin knife between the collar and soufflé to separate. Remove clip or pin, hold end of collar and pull carefully to remove.

★ SPECIAL—AND WORTH IT

Sugared Orange Soufflé

2 tablespoons plus ½ cup granulated sugar
⅓ cup all-purpose flour
1 cup half-and-half or milk
2 teaspoons *each* grated fresh orange and lemon peel
⅓ cup orange-flavor liqueur or thawed orange-juice concentrate
6 large eggs, separated
⅛ teaspoon cream of tartar
Confectioners' sugar
Whipped cream (optional)

1. Heat oven to 375°F. Heavily grease a 1½-quart soufflé dish fitted with a collar (see Making a Soufflé Collar, at left). Sprinkle 2 tablespoons of the granulated sugar into soufflé dish and shake to coat dish and collar evenly.

2. Put flour in a medium-size saucepan (preferably nonstick). Stir in half-and-half until blended. Cook over high heat, stirring constantly, until thickened and smooth. Cook 1 minute, stirring constantly. Remove from heat. Stir in peels and liqueur.

3. Beat egg yolks into flour mixture one at a time, beating well after each.

4. Beat egg whites and cream of tartar with an electric mixer at high speed until foamy. Gradually beat in remaining ½ cup granulated sugar, 1 tablespoon at a time, until mixture forms glossy moist peaks when beaters are lifted.

5. Stir one fourth of the whites into sauce to lighten it. Pour sauce over remaining whites. Fold together with a rubber spatula until almost completely blended.

6. Pour mixture into prepared soufflé dish. Smooth top with spatula.

7. Bake 30 to 35 minutes, until center is firm.

8. Gently remove collar. Sprinkle soufflé with confectioners' sugar and serve immediately with whipped cream, if desired.

Makes 6 servings. Per serving (made with half-and-half and liqueur, without whipped cream): 267 calories, 8 grams protein, 29 grams carbohydrate, 11 grams fat, 209 milligrams cholesterol, 80 milligrams sodium

Cold Lemon Soufflé

(Shown on page 79)

A classy and refreshing dessert.

- **3 envelopes unflavored gelatin**
- **¾ cup cold water**
- **1 cup boiling water**
- **¾ cup granulated sugar**
- **2 tablespoons grated fresh lemon peel**
- **1 cup fresh-squeezed lemon juice**
- **2 containers (15 ounces each) part-skim ricotta cheese (3¼ cups)**
- **2 tablespoons meringue powder and ½ cup cold water, or whites from 4 large eggs, at room temperature, and ½ teaspoon cream of tartar (see Egg Safety, page 57)**
- **For garnish: ⅓ cup toasted sliced almonds; 1 small lemon, halved and thinly sliced; and a mint sprig**

1. Have ready a 1-quart soufflé dish with a collar (see Making a Soufflé Collar, page 85) or a 1½-quart serving bowl.

2. Sprinkle gelatin over cold water in a large bowl. Let stand 1 minute to soften. Add boiling water and stir 3 minutes, until gelatin is completely dissolved and liquid looks clear.

3. Add ½ cup of the sugar and the lemon peel and juice to the gelatin mixture and stir until sugar dissolves.

4. Refrigerate about 1 hour, stirring three times, until mixture thickens to the consistency of unbeaten egg whites and mounds slightly when dropped from a spoon.

5. Process ricotta in a food processor or a blender until smooth and creamy. Stir into lemon mixture.

6. Beat meringue powder and cold water (or egg whites and cream of tartar) with an electric mixer at high speed until foamy. Gradually add remaining ¼ cup sugar and beat until stiff peaks form when beaters are lifted.

7. Fold beaten meringue powder into gelatin mixture with a rubber spatula until completely blended.

8. Pour mixture into prepared soufflé dish or serving bowl. Cover loosely and chill 3 hours, until completely set.

9. To serve from soufflé dish: Gently remove the collar. Carefully press almonds onto exposed sides of soufflé. Garnish the top with lemon slices and mint sprig. To serve from bowl: Omit nuts. Garnish with lemon slices and mint. Spoon soufflé onto serving plates.

Makes 10 servings. Per serving with meringue powder (without garnish): 196 calories, 13 grams protein, 22 grams carbohydrate, 7 grams fat, 22 milligrams cholesterol, 131 milligrams sodium

Beating Egg Whites

☐ Stiffly beaten egg whites are often incorporated into soufflé mixtures to lighten texture and to make hot soufflés rise.

☐ Yolks and whites are most easily separated when eggs are very cold, but whites can be beaten to greater volume when they're at room temperature. Crack open eggs one at a time, letting the whites drop into a small perfectly clean bowl, yolks into another small bowl. Check the whites and scoop out any tiny bit of yolk with an egg shell (the tiniest bit of grease or egg yolk will keep them from beating properly). Pour into mixing bowl. Cover yolks and whites and let warm to room temperature.

☐ Beat whites just until they hold low, distinct, moist peaks. Overbeating makes them dry and lumpy; underbeating prevents the soufflé from rising as high as possible.

Left to right: Plum Yogurt Snow, Apricot Yogurt Snow, Cold Raspberry Soufflé

🕐 **MAKE-AHEAD**
★ **SPECIAL—AND WORTH IT**

Cold Raspberry Soufflé

Instead of spooning the soufflé into ramekins, you may serve it in stemmed glasses.

> 3 **envelopes unflavored gelatin**
> ½ **cup cold water**
> 4 **cups (about 4 half-pint baskets)**
> **fresh or frozen unsweetened**
> **raspberries**
> ¼ **cup raspberry jelly or preserves**
> ⅓ **cup granulated sugar**
> ½ **cup unsweetened applesauce**
> 1¼ **cups (8 ounces) part-skim ricotta**
> **cheese**
> 2 **tablespoons meringue powder and**
> ½ **cup cold water, or whites from**
> **4 large eggs, at room**
> **temperature, and ½ teaspoon**
> **cream of tartar (see Egg Safety,**
> **page 57)**
> **For garnish: ¼ cup coarsely chopped**
> **toasted hazelnuts, plain low-fat**
> **yogurt and 6 raspberries**

1. Put collars on six ½-cup ramekins (see Making a Soufflé Collar, page 85).

2. Sprinkle gelatin over water in a small bowl. Let stand 2 minutes to soften.

3. Mix raspberries, jelly and half the sugar in a medium-size saucepan (not uncoated aluminum). Bring to a boil over medium heat, stirring

often. Add softened gelatin, remove from heat and stir 3 minutes, until gelatin is completely dissolved. Let cool 5 minutes.

4. Press raspberry mixture through a strainer suspended over a large bowl to remove seeds; discard seeds (you should have about 2 cups mixture).

5. Stir applesauce into raspberry mixture. Refrigerate about 1 hour, stirring three times, until mixture thickens to the consistency of unbeaten egg whites and mounds slightly when dropped from a spoon.

6. Process ricotta in a food processor or a blender until smooth and creamy. Stir into raspberry mixture.

7. Beat meringue powder and water (or egg whites and cream of tartar) with an electric mixer on high speed until foamy. Gradually add remaining sugar and beat until stiff peaks form when beaters are lifted.

8. Fold beaten meringue powder into raspberry mixture until completely blended. Spoon into prepared ramekins. Cover loosely and chill 3 hours, until completely set.

9. To serve: Carefully remove collars. To garnish: Carefully press hazelnuts onto exposed sides of soufflés. Top each with a dollop of yogurt and a raspberry and serve.

Makes 6 servings. Per serving (with meringue powder): 216 calories, 11 grams protein, 37 grams carbohydrate, 4 grams fat, 12 milligrams cholesterol, 90 milligrams sodium

★ SPECIAL—AND WORTH IT

Rum-Praline Soufflé

Pass praline powder to spoon over servings.

**2 tablespoons plus ⅔ cup
    granulated sugar**
1 cup half-and-half or milk
⅓ cup all-purpose flour
6 large eggs, separated
¼ cup dark rum
⅛ teaspoon cream of tartar
⅓ cup Praline Powder (recipe follows)
Lightly whipped cream (optional)

1. Heat oven to 375°F. Heavily grease a 1½-quart soufflé dish fitted with a foil collar (see Making a Soufflé Collar, page 85). Dust with 2 tablespoons of the sugar and shake dish to coat evenly.

2. Pour half-and-half into a medium-size saucepan (preferably nonstick). Stir in flour until blended. Cook over high heat, stirring constantly, until thickened and smooth. Cook 1 minute, stirring constantly. Remove from heat.

3. Add ⅓ cup of the sugar to flour mixture and stir until dissolved.

4. Add egg yolks to flour mixture one at a time, beating well after each. Stir in rum until blended and set aside.

5. Beat egg whites and cream of tartar with an electric mixer on high speed until foamy. Gradually beat in remaining ⅓ cup sugar, about 1 tablespoon at a time, until whites form stiff moist peaks when beaters are lifted.

6. Stir one fourth of the whites into sauce to lighten it, then scrape sauce over remaining whites. Fold in gently with a rubber spatula until mixture is almost completely blended. Fold in ⅓ cup Praline Powder.

7. Pour mixture into prepared dish and smooth top with spatula.

8. Bake 30 to 35 minutes, until center is firm.

9. Gently remove collar. Serve immediately with whipped cream, if desired.

Makes 6 servings. Per serving (made with half-and-half, without whipped cream): 233 calories, 10 grams protein, 11 grams carbohydrate, 14 grams fat, 209 milligrams cholesterol, 80 milligrams sodium

Praline Powder

¾ cup granulated sugar
¾ cup sliced almonds

1. Grease a 12-inch-long piece of foil. Put foil greased-side up on a baking sheet.

2. Melt sugar in a medium-size heavy skillet over low heat, stirring occasionally, until sugar turns syrupy and is golden brown. Remove from heat. (Be careful; sugar is extremely hot.)

3. Stir almonds into the hot syrup. Scrape mixture onto prepared foil. Set aside until completely cool and hard.

4. Remove from foil and break praline into small pieces with a rolling pin or a heavy knife. Pulverize mixture to a powder in a dry food processor or blender. (If the food processor is wet, it will melt the praline.) Store in an airtight container until ready to use.

Makes about 1⅓ cups.

Note: Don't make this on a humid day; it won't harden properly.

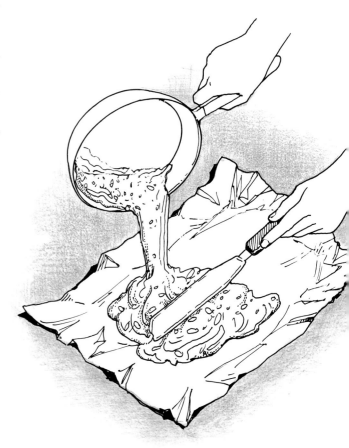

Cocoa-Espresso Soufflé

Almost like a hot fudge brownie, this special dessert is wonderful served with small scoops of coffee ice cream.

⅔ cup granulated sugar
⅓ cup unsweetened cocoa powder
¼ cup powdered instant espresso coffee
3 tablespoons cornstarch
¾ cup milk
¼ cup butter or margarine
1 teaspoon vanilla extract
4 large eggs, separated
¼ teaspoon cream of tartar

1. Put one rack in bottom position of oven. Heat oven to 375°F. Heavily grease a 1½-quart soufflé dish fitted with a 2-inch foil collar (see Making a Soufflé Collar, page 85).

2. Mix ⅓ cup of the sugar, the cocoa, espresso powder and cornstarch in a medium-size heavy saucepan. Gradually stir in milk until smooth. Cook over medium heat, stirring constantly, until mixture is thickened and smooth. Remove from heat.

3. Stir butter and vanilla into hot cocoa mixture until butter is melted and blended. Add egg yolks one at a time, beating well after each.

4. Beat egg whites with an electric mixer on high speed until foamy. Add cream of tartar and continue beating, gradually adding remaining ⅓ cup sugar, until mixture forms stiff moist peaks when beaters are lifted.

5. Stir one fourth of the whites into the chocolate mixture to lighten it.

6. Scrape chocolate mixture over the remaining whites. Fold in gently with a rubber spatula until blended.

7. Scrape into prepared dish. Bake on bottom oven rack 30 to 35 minutes, until center is firm.

8. Gently remove collar from soufflé and serve immediately.

Makes 6 servings. Per serving: 176 calories, 6 grams protein, 29 grams carbohydrate, 5 grams fat, 129 milligrams cholesterol with butter, 105 milligrams cholesterol with margarine, 48 milligrams sodium

Chocolate Soufflé

For best flavor, use a good-quality chocolate.

2 tablespoons plus ½ cup granulated sugar
4 ounces semisweet chocolate, broken in small pieces
⅓ cup water
1 tablespoon instant-coffee granules
⅓ cup all-purpose flour
1 cup milk
½ teaspoon vanilla extract
6 large eggs, separated
⅛ teaspoon cream of tartar
Confectioners' sugar

1. Heat oven to 375°F. Heavily grease a 1½-quart soufflé dish fitted with a foil collar (see Making a Soufflé Collar, page 85). Sprinkle 2 tablespoons of the granulated sugar into soufflé dish and shake to coat dish and collar evenly.

2. Put chocolate, water and coffee granules in a small saucepan. Melt chocolate over low heat until smooth, stirring occasionally. Remove from heat.

3. Put flour in a medium-size heavy saucepan (preferably nonstick). Stir in milk until blended. Cook over high heat, stirring constantly, until thickened and smooth. Cook 1 minute, stirring constantly. Remove from heat.

4. Stir vanilla and the chocolate mixture into flour mixture.

5. Beat egg yolks into flour mixture one at a time, beating well after each.

6. Beat egg whites and cream of tartar with an electric mixer on high speed until foamy. Gradually add remaining ½ cup granulated sugar, 1 tablespoon at a time, until mixture forms glossy moist peaks when beaters are lifted.

7. Stir one fourth of the whites into sauce to lighten it. Pour sauce over remaining whites. Fold together with a rubber spatula until almost completely blended.

8. Pour mixture into prepared soufflé dish. Smooth the top with spatula.

9. Bake 30 to 35 minutes, until center is firm.

10. Gently remove the collar. Sprinkle soufflé with confectioners' sugar and serve immediately.

Makes 6 servings. Per serving: 272 calories, 9 grams protein, 29 grams carbohydrate, 14 grams fat, 298 milligrams cholesterol, 88 milligrams sodium

Cold Chocolate Soufflé

Cold Chocolate Soufflé

  1 **envelope plus 1 teaspoon unflavored gelatin**
  ½ **cup cold water**
  ½ **cup nonfat dry-milk powder**
  ⅔ **cup confectioners' sugar**
  ½ **cup unsweetened cocoa powder**
  ⅔ **cup skim milk**
  1¼ **cups (7½ ounces) semisweet**
      chocolate chips
  1 **container (15 ounces) part-skim**
      ricotta cheese
  1 **teaspoon vanilla extract**
  ¼ **teaspoon almond extract**
  3 **tablespoons meringue powder and ¾ cup cold**
      water, or whites from 8 large eggs, at room
      temperature (see Egg Safety, page 57)
For garnish: additional ¼ cup confectioners' sugar

1. Have ready a 1-quart soufflé dish or eight ½-cup ramekins. Make collar for soufflé dish or for the ramekins (see Making a Soufflé Collar, page 85). Lightly oil the inside of dish and collar.

2. Sprinkle gelatin over water in a small bowl. Let stand 2 minutes.

3. Mix milk powder, ½ cup of the confectioners' sugar and the cocoa in a small heavy saucepan until well blended. Add skim milk and gelatin mixture and stir until well blended (mixture will still be grainy).

4. Heat mixture over low heat 4 to 5 minutes, stirring often, until mixture is smooth and steam begins to rise. (Do not boil.) Remove from heat. Immediately stir in chocolate chips.

5. Cover and let stand about 5 minutes, stirring occasionally, until chocolate chips melt. Pour into a large bowl and let cool almost to room temperature.

6. Meanwhile, purée ricotta and extracts in a food processor or a blender until smooth.

7. Beat meringue powder and water (or egg whites) with an electric mixer on high speed until soft peaks form. Gradually beat in remaining confectioners' sugar (except ¼ cup for garnish) until stiff peaks form when beaters are lifted.

8. Stir ricotta mixture into chocolate mixture. Fold in beaten meringue powder until well blended.

9. Pour into prepared soufflé dish or spoon into ramekins. Refrigerate large soufflé at least 4 hours, ramekins 2 hours, until completely set.

10. Just before serving, gently peel off collar. Place paper doily on top of soufflé. Dust generously with confectioners' sugar; carefully lift off doily.

11. Spoon large soufflé onto serving plates or serve individual soufflés from ramekins.

Makes 8 servings. Per serving (with meringue powder): 271 calories, 12 grams protein, 33 grams carbohydrate, 13 grams fat, 10 milligrams cholesterol, 120 milligrams sodium

Frozen Desserts

Whip up a fruity sorbetto or ice. Get out the ice-cream freezer and churn the richest ice cream ever. Or relive childhood pleasures with a slimmed-down banana split.

Left to right: Espresso, Vanilla and Chocolate Gelato

Ice Cream

🕐 **MAKE-AHEAD**
★ **SPECIAL—AND WORTH IT**

Vanilla Gelato

You will need an ice-cream freezer for this.

2 cups half-and-half
1 vanilla bean, split lengthwise (see Vanilla, page 61), or 2 teaspoons vanilla extract
Yolks from 4 large eggs, at room temperature
⅔ cup granulated sugar

1. Slowly heat half-and-half and vanilla bean in a medium-size heavy saucepan over medium-low heat until boiling. Remove from heat, cover and let stand 5 minutes.

2. Remove vanilla bean; when cool enough to handle, scrape the seeds into the half-and-half.

3. Beat egg yolks and sugar with an electric mixer on high speed until pale and fluffy. With mixer on low speed, slowly pour the hot half-and-half into the yolk mixture. Return combined mixture to saucepan.

4. Cook over low heat (do not boil), whisking constantly, until mixture thickens slightly, coats a metal spoon and registers 160°F on a candy or instant-read thermometer.

5. Strain mixture into a clean bowl. Set bowl in a larger bowl filled halfway with ice water. If using vanilla extract, stir in now. Let mixture cool to room temperature, stirring occasionally.

6. Refrigerate at least 1 hour.

7. Freeze in an ice-cream freezer according to manufacturer's directions.

Gelato

It sounds exotic, but it's actually very familiar. *Gelato* is the Italian word for ice cream, but Italians prefer their ice cream smoother and denser than their American counterparts do. For these recipes you'll need an ice-cream freezer and a candy or instant-read thermometer. Once made, gelato can be frozen in an airtight container up to a week. Remove to refrigerator 30 minutes before serving or until soft enough to spoon.

---

8. Serve immediately or freeze in an airtight container up to 1 week.

Makes 3 cups. Per ½ cup: 232 calories, 4 grams protein, 26 grams carbohydrate, 13 grams fat, 162 milligrams cholesterol, 43 milligrams sodium

🕐 **MAKE-AHEAD**
★ **SPECIAL—AND WORTH IT**

Chocolate Gelato

Look for bittersweet chocolate in the gourmet-chocolate section of your market. Semisweet chocolate can be substituted, but the gelato will be somewhat sweeter. The better-quality the chocolate, the more delicious your dessert will be. You will need an ice-cream freezer.

1 cup water
½ cup granulated sugar
Yolks from 8 large eggs, at room temperature
1 pound bittersweet chocolate, broken up, melted and cooled to lukewarm (see Melting Chocolate, page 48)
2 cups half-and-half

1. Stir water and sugar in a large heavy saucepan over medium heat until sugar dissolves. Raise heat to high and bring to a boil. Remove from heat. Pour sugar syrup into a glass measure for easier handling.

2. Beat egg yolks with an electric mixer on high speed until pale and fluffy. Beating on low speed, slowly pour hot sugar mixture into egg yolks. Return combined mixture to saucepan.

3. Cook over low heat (do not boil), whisking constantly, until mixture thickens slightly, coats a metal spoon and registers 160°F on a candy or instant-read thermometer. Remove from heat and stir in melted chocolate until blended.

4. Transfer to a clean bowl. Set bowl in a larger bowl filled halfway with ice water. Let mixture cool to room temperature, stirring occasionally. Stir in half-and-half.

5. Refrigerate at least 1 hour.

6. Freeze in an ice-cream freezer according to manufacturer's directions.

7. Serve immediately or freeze in an airtight container up to 1 week.

Makes 1½ quarts (6 cups). Per ½ cup: 305 calories, 6 grams protein, 28 grams carbohydrate, 23 grams fat, 144 milligrams cholesterol, 26 milligrams sodium

Chocolate-Hazelnut Gelato

3 tablespoons unsweetened cocoa
    powder, sifted
3 cups half-and-half
Yolks from 6 large eggs, at room
    temperature
⅔ cup granulated sugar
½ cup hazelnuts, toasted, skinned and
    finely ground (see Note)

1. Put cocoa in a medium-size heavy saucepan. Stir in a little half-and-half until smooth. Slowly stir in remaining half-and-half. Place over medium heat and bring to a boil. Remove from heat.

2. Beat egg yolks and sugar with an electric mixer on high speed until pale and fluffy. Beating on low speed, slowly pour hot cocoa mixture into yolk mixture. Return combined mixture to saucepan.

3. Cook over low heat (do not boil), whisking constantly, until mixture thickens slightly, coats a metal spoon and registers 160°F on a candy or instant-read thermometer.

4. Strain mixture into a clean medium-size bowl. Set bowl in a larger bowl filled halfway with ice water. Let cool to room temperature, stirring occasionally.

5. Stir ground hazelnuts into cocoa mixture. Cover and refrigerate at least 1 hour.

6. Freeze in an ice-cream freezer according to manufacturer's directions.

7. Serve immediately or freeze in an airtight container up to 1 week.

Makes 1 quart (4 cups). Per ½ cup: 280 calories, 6 grams protein, 23 grams carbohydrate, 19 grams fat, 182 milligrams cholesterol, 49 milligrams sodium

Note: Spread nuts in a shallow pan. Toast in a 350°F oven 15 minutes, until skins split and nuts begin to brown. (You may also toast the nuts in your microwave oven; see Microwave Tips for Desserts, page 33.) Turn out onto a clean kitchen towel and rub the nuts between folds of the towel to remove most of the skins. Let cool. Pick out nuts. Some of the brown skins will remain attached; this is okay. Process nuts in a food processor or a blender until finely ground, being careful not to grind nuts to an oily paste.

Espresso Gelato
(Shown on page 92)

Make espresso by dissolving 2 rounded teaspoons instant espresso powder in ¾ cup water.

¾ cup very strong espresso coffee
½ cup granulated sugar
Yolks from 8 large eggs, at room
    temperature
½ cup heavy cream, whipped to
    soft peaks

1. Stir espresso and sugar in a medium-size heavy saucepan over medium-low heat until sugar dissolves. Raise heat to high and bring to a boil. Remove from heat.

2. Beat egg yolks with an electric mixer on high speed until pale and fluffy. Beating on low speed, slowly pour hot espresso mixture into the yolks. Return combined mixture to saucepan.

3. Cook over low heat (do not boil), whisking constantly, until mixture thickens, coats a metal spoon and registers 160°F on a candy or instant-read thermometer.

4. Strain yolk mixture into a clean bowl. Place bowl in a larger bowl filled halfway with ice water. Let yolk mixture cool to room temperature, stirring occasionally.

5. Fold in whipped cream. Refrigerate at least 1 hour.

6. Freeze in an ice-cream freezer according to manufacturer's directions.

7. Serve immediately or freeze in an airtight container up to 1 week.

Makes 3 cups. Per ½ cup: 213 calories, 4 grams protein, 17 grams carbohydrate, 14 grams fat, 281 milligrams cholesterol, 18 milligrams sodium

Chocolate Ice Cream

A dessert that is a chocolate-lover's delight. Best of all, you don't need an ice cream freezer to prepare this delicious version of an all-time favorite.

⅔ cup granulated sugar
½ cup unsweetened cocoa powder
2 cups half-and-half
1 teaspoon vanilla extract

1. Mix sugar and cocoa in a small saucepan. Gradually stir in ½ cup of the half-and-half until smooth. Cook over low heat about 5 minutes, stirring frequently, until sugar and cocoa dissolve. Remove from heat.

2. Stir in remaining 1½ cups half-and-half and the vanilla until well blended.

3. Freeze in an ice-cream freezer according to manufacturer's directions. If you don't have an ice-cream freezer, pour into an 8-inch square metal pan and put in freezer. When frozen about 1 inch around sides of pan but still slushy in center, stir well. Cover and freeze until almost firm. In a chilled bowl with chilled beaters, beat ice cream with an electric mixer on medium speed until smooth and thick. Return to pan. Stir twice during first hour, then cover and freeze until firm.

4. To soften hard-frozen ice cream: Place in refrigerator 15 minutes to soften before serving.

Makes 4 servings. Per serving: 318 calories, 6 grams protein, 44 grams carbohydrate, 16 grams fat, 52 milligrams cholesterol, 57 milligrams sodium

🕐 MAKE-AHEAD
★ SPECIAL—AND WORTH IT

Old-fashioned Custard Ice Cream

The real thing—rich, creamy and delicious. If you don't have an ice cream freezer, you can make this in a pan in the freezer.

2 cups milk
¾ cup granulated sugar
1 tablespoon cornstarch
¼ teaspoon salt
2 large eggs
2 cups heavy cream
1 tablespoon vanilla extract

1. Heat milk in a medium-size heavy saucepan over medium heat just until small bubbles form around the edges. Remove from heat.

2. Mix sugar, cornstarch and salt in a medium-size bowl. Gradually stir in milk until smooth. Return to saucepan.

3. Cook mixture over low heat 10 minutes, stirring constantly, until slightly thickened. Remove from heat.

4. Beat eggs in same bowl with a wire whisk. Gradually beat ½ cup of the hot milk mixture into eggs. Return to saucepan. Cook about 2 minutes, stirring constantly, until mixture thickens, coats a metal spoon and registers 160°F on a candy or instant-read thermometer. Remove from heat.

5. Refrigerate until cool. Stir in heavy cream and vanilla.

6. Freeze in an ice-cream freezer according to manufacturer's directions. If you don't have an ice-cream freezer, pour into a 9-inch square metal pan. Freeze about 2 hours, until partially frozen. Turn into a chilled metal bowl and beat until smooth with a whisk or an electric mixer. Cover and freeze until firm.

7. Serve immediately or freeze in an airtight container up to 1 week.

Makes 1½ quarts. Per ½ cup: 230 calories, 3 grams protein, 16 grams carbohydrate, 17 grams fat, 60 milligrams cholesterol, 88 milligrams sodium

Pumpkin-Toffee Ice Cream

Woman's Day has helped get Thanksgiving dinner on the table ever since November 1937, when Kitchen Director Cora Anthony based the whole menu on native American foods. Get out the ice-cream freezer for Miss Anthony's dessert, which we made with toffee instead of the pecans in the original recipe. The ice cream will have a slightly grainy texture because of the pumpkin.

 2 large eggs
 1 can (16 ounces) solid-pack
     pumpkin
 1 cup milk
 1 cup packed brown sugar
1½ teaspoons ground cinnamon
     (see Note)
 1 teaspoon ground ginger
 ¼ teaspoon ground cloves
 ¼ teaspoon salt
1½ cups half-and-half
 3 chocolate-covered toffee bars (1.4
     or 1.20 ounces each), finely
     chopped (¾ cup)

1. Lighty beat eggs in a large bowl with a wire whisk.

2. Mix pumpkin, milk, sugar, spices and salt in a large heavy saucepan. Stir over medium-low heat until hot. Remove from heat.

3. Gradually stir about ½ cup of the hot pumpkin mixture into the eggs until blended. Add to saucepan and stir over low heat about 3 minutes, until mixture registers 160°F on a candy or instant-read thermometer. Remove from heat.

4. Transfer to a large clean bowl and stir in half-and-half. Partially cover with plastic wrap and refrigerate until completely cool.

5. Freeze in an ice-cream freezer according to manufacturer's directions. When mixture starts to stiffen, about 2 to 4 minutes before it's firm, add chopped toffee. Continue freezing until toffee is evenly distributed and ice cream is ready.

6. Serve immediately or transfer to a 1½-quart freezer container, cover tightly and store in freezer.

Makes 5 cups. Per ½ cup: 244 calories, 5 grams protein, 34 grams carbohydrate, 7 grams fat, 58 milligrams cholesterol, 139 milligrams sodium

Note: You can use 2 teaspoons pumpkin-pie spice instead of the cinnamon, ginger and cloves.

Microwave Method: Assemble first seven ingredients in a 2-quart microwave-safe casserole. Cover with a lid or vented plastic wrap. Microwave on high 4 to 5 minutes, stirring and rotating dish twice, until hot. Stir ½ cup of the mixture into eggs, then add to casserole. Cover; microwave on medium-high 2 to 3 minutes, until mixture registers 160°F on a candy or instant-read thermometer. Proceed as directed.

Pumpkin-Toffee Ice Cream

Coco-Loco Ice Cream with Fruit

Prepare the ice-cream mixture a day ahead, chill overnight, then freeze in an ice-cream freezer according to manufacturer's directions.

ICE CREAM

1 envelope unflavored gelatin
¼ cup water
2 cups light cream or half-and-half
1½ cups heavy cream
½ cup granulated sugar
1 can (8½ ounces) cream of coconut

FRUIT

1 ripe kiwifruit, peeled, halved
    lengthwise, then thinly sliced
    crosswise
1 cup canned apricot nectar

1. To make ice cream: Sprinkle gelatin over water in a medium-size saucepan. Let stand 1 minute to soften. Stir over low heat about 3 minutes, scraping down sides occasionally, until liquid is almost boiling and gelatin is completely dissolved.

2. Stir light and heavy creams and the sugar into the gelatin mixture. Cook over low heat, stirring often, until mixture simmers and sugar is dissolved. Remove from heat and pour into a medium-size bowl. Let cool to room temperature.

3. Stir cream of coconut into gelatin mixture. Cover and refrigerate overnight.

4. Stir cream mixture well. Freeze in an ice-cream freezer according to manufacturer's directions.

5. To serve: Place 2 scoops ice cream in each of eight dessert glasses. Top with kiwifruit slices, then pour 2 tablespoons apricot nectar over each.

Makes 1 quart ice cream; 8 servings. Per serving (with light cream): 436 calories, 4 grams protein, 42 grams carbohydrate, 29 grams fat, 85 milligrams cholesterol, 53 milligrams sodium

Mango Ice Cream

Thin slices of lime, mango or star fruit make beautiful garnishes.

2 large ripe mangoes, peeled and cut
    up (about 2½ cups)
½ cup thawed frozen cholesterol-free
    egg product
½ cup granulated sugar
Pinch of salt
½ cup light corn syrup
1 cup heavy cream
1 cup milk
2 tablespoons plus 2 teaspoons fresh
    lime juice

1. Purée mangoes in a food processor or a blender until smooth (you should have about 2½ cups purée).

2. Beat egg product, sugar and salt in a large bowl with a wire whisk until sugar is dissolved. Beat in mango purée, corn syrup, heavy cream, milk and lime juice until well blended.

3. Pour into a 13x9-inch metal pan. Freeze about 3 hours until almost firm.

4. Beat mixture smooth with an electric mixer on medium-high speed. Freeze until almost firm and beat again.

5. Pack into a freezer container. Cover and freeze until firm.

6. Let soften in refrigerator a few minutes before serving.

Makes about 8 cups. Per ½ cup: 130 calories, 2 grams protein, 20 grams carbohydrate, 6 grams fat, 22 milligrams cholesterol, 42 milligrams sodium

Mango Ice Cream

Speedy Strawberry Semifreddo

Frozen sweetened strawberries, raspberries or peaches can be whipped in a blender or a food processor with a little cream to make instant *semifreddo* (which means half-cold in Italian). Semifreddos—desserts served partially frozen—are generally made of whipped cream. Serve plain or with fresh or canned fruit, or as a sauce for poached pears and other fruits. The recipe can easily be doubled to serve four.

1 package (10 ounces) frozen quick-
**   thaw strawberries in syrup**
¼ cup heavy cream

1. Open packet of strawberries and cut in 12 cubes. Put cubes and cream in a food processor or a blender. Process about 1 minute, stopping machine once to scrape down sides, until mixture is smooth and reaches the consistency of soft ice cream.

2. Spoon into two chilled bowls and serve immediately.

Makes 1⅓ cups; 2 servings. Per serving: 260 calories, 1 gram protein, 40 grams carbohydrate, 11 grams fat, 40 milligrams cholesterol, 11 milligrams sodium

Strawberry and Cream Freeze

Only four ingredients. No ice-cream freezer needed, but it tastes just like rich ice cream.

3 cups thinly sliced fresh strawberries
¼ cup plus 2 tablespoons granulated
**   sugar**
2 cups heavy cream
1 teaspoon vanilla extract

1. Mash strawberries with ¼ cup of the sugar in a large bowl with a pastry blender or a potato masher until almost puréed but still chunky. Or pulse briefly in a food processor.

2. Beat cream, remaining 2 tablespoons sugar and the vanilla with an electric mixer on high speed until stiff peaks form when beaters are lifted. Fold in berries with a rubber spatula just until blended.

3. Spoon into eight dessert dishes or 6-ounce ramekins. Place in a large metal pan for easy handling. Cover entire pan with foil or cover individual dishes. Put pan in freezer, making sure it is level. Freeze overnight, until firm, or up to 1 week.

4. Let soften about 5 minutes at room temperature before serving.

Makes 8 servings. Per serving: 254 calories, 1 gram protein, 13 grams carbohydrate, 23 grams fat, 79 milligrams cholesterol, 19 milligrams sodium

⏱ **MAKE-AHEAD**

Super Easy Orange Chocolate-Chip Ice-Cream Mold

Use any shape mold you want. Or freeze the ice cream in the bowl; it will have a pretty domed shape when unmolded. Serve with a warm chocolate sauce (see Sauce chapter) or with lightly whipped cream, or sprinkle the dessert with grated bittersweet chocolate.

2 cups heavy cream
½ cup granulated sugar
½ cup thawed frozen orange-juice
**   concentrate**
½ cup semisweet chocolate mini-chips
For garnish: orange slices cut in
**   quarters**

1. Place a 3-cup mold in the refrigerator to chill.

2. Stir cream, sugar and orange-juice concentrate in a medium-size metal bowl until sugar dissolves.

3. Place in freezer 1½ hours, until partially frozen (mixture must be thick so that chips won't sink).

4. Fold chocolate chips into cream mixture. Pour into chilled mold. Cover and freeze until firm, several hours or overnight.

5. To unmold: Run the tip of a sharp knife around the rim of mold. Place upside-down on a serving platter, but don't remove mold. Refrigerate 30 minutes, until the mold can be lifted and removed. Garnish with a border of orange slices, then return to freezer until serving time.

6. To serve: Slice mold and put on six dessert plates or spoon into bowls.

Makes 6 servings. Per serving: 455 calories, 3 grams protein, 37 grams carbohydrate, 35 grams fat, 106 milligrams cholesterol, 26 milligrams sodium

Plum-Almond Tortoni

5. Spoon about ⅓ cup of the mixture into each baking cup. Sprinkle each with ¼ teaspoon of the remaining crumbs. Freeze about 2 hours, until firm, or up to 1 week.

6. Let soften a few minutes in refrigerator before serving.

Makes 8 servings. Per serving (with brandy): 230 calories, 2 grams protein, 25 grams carbohydrate, 15 grams fat, 55 milligrams cholesterol, 33 milligrams sodium

Note: If desired, substitute additional lemon juice for the brandy.

Slim Banana Split
(Shown on page 64)

To cut the calorie count dramatically, we made the chocolate sauce with cocoa and buttermilk instead of chocolate and cream. Bottled strawberry topping is replaced with sweetened strawberries, and the ice cream with frozen yogurt.

⅓ **cup unsweetened cocoa powder**
¼ **cup packed light-brown sugar**
½ **cup buttermilk**
 1 **cup fresh strawberries, rinsed,**
    drained, hulled and finely chopped
 1 **teaspoon granulated sugar**
 2 **medium-size bananas, each split**
    lengthwise, then cut in half
    crosswise
 1 **pint frozen low-fat vanilla yogurt**
 4 **maraschino cherries (optional)**

1. Mix cocoa and brown sugar in a small heavy saucepan. Add buttermilk and cook over medium-low heat 3 to 4 minutes, stirring constantly, until sugar melts and mixture is smooth. Remove from heat and let cool.

2. Toss strawberries with granulated sugar in a small bowl.

3. To assemble: Place 2 pieces banana in each of four dessert dishes. Add 2 scoops frozen yogurt. Spoon on 1 tablespoon of the chocolate sauce and 3 tablespoons of the strawberry sauce. Top each with a cherry, if desired.

Makes 4 servings. Per serving (with cherries): 210 calories, 5 grams protein, 46 grams carbohydrate, 2 grams fat, 4 milligrams cholesterol, 13 milligrams sodium

⏱ **MAKE-AHEAD**
Plum-Almond Tortoni

To make crumbs quickly, break up cookies and process in a blender or a food processor.

½ **cup plum jam or preserves**
 4 **teaspoons brandy (see Note)**
 1 **tablespoon fresh-squeezed**
    lemon juice
⅛ **teaspoon vanilla extract**
Pinch of salt
 1 **cup heavy cream**
⅓ **cup plus 2 teaspoons crisp amaretti**
    crumbs (from about 6 cookies)

1. Line a muffin tin with eight 2½-inch paper-lined foil baking cups.

2. Stir jam, brandy, lemon juice, vanilla and salt in a small bowl until blended.

3. Beat cream with an electric mixer on high speed until soft peaks form when beaters are lifted.

4. Gently fold jam mixture and ⅓ cup of the crumbs into the cream.

Sorbets and Ices

🕐 MAKE-AHEAD

Cantaloupe-and-Cream Ice

You need a food processor to make this.

> 1 medium-size ripe cantaloupe (2½ to 2¾ pounds), halved, seeded and rind cut off
> ¼ cup granulated sugar
> ½ cup heavy cream

1. Cut melon in small thin pieces (you should have about 6 cups). Divide evenly between two large zipper-closure freezer bags. Add half the sugar to each and shake to mix. Squeeze out the air, seal bags and lay flat in freezer. Freeze until hard, at least 3 hours or overnight.

2. Bend bags a few times to separate melon pieces. Process with cream in two batches in a food processor until smooth.

3. Serve immediately or spoon into a freezer container, seal tightly and freeze up to 1 week. Let soften in refrigerator 30 minutes before serving.

Makes 6 servings, ⅔ cup each. Per serving: 158 calories, 1 gram protein, 23 grams carbohydrate, 8 grams fat, 27 milligrams cholesterol, 29 milligrams sodium

Cantaloupe-and-Cream Ice

🕐 MAKE-AHEAD
✳ MICROWAVE

Cranberry Ice

For Thanksgiving, make this refreshing ice instead of the traditional cranberry sauce. For a change, substitute orange juice for some or all of the water. Freeze the ice in a clean milk carton and serve it sliced or scooped.

> 1 bag (12 ounces) fresh or frozen cranberries (3 cups), rinsed and drained
> 2½ cups water
> 1½ cups granulated sugar
> 2 tablespoons fresh-squeezed lemon juice

1. Bring cranberries and 1½ cups of the water to a boil in a medium-size saucepan (not uncoated aluminum) over high heat. Reduce heat to medium-low and simmer 5 to 7 minutes, until cranberries are tender. Remove from heat and let cool slightly.

2. Put cranberries through a food mill or press through a strainer suspended over a medium-size bowl (you should have about 2½ cups purée). Discard skin and seeds.

3. In same saucepan, mix sugar and remaining 1 cup water. Bring to a boil over high heat. Boil 5 minutes, until mixture is a thin syrup. Remove from heat. Stir in lemon juice and cranberry purée.

4. Pour into a clean 1-quart milk carton or plastic freezer container. Freeze several hours or overnight, until firm.

5. To serve: Cut away milk carton and let stand 10 minutes before slicing or scooping.

Makes 4 cups; 8 servings. Per ½ cup: 164 calories, 0 grams protein, 42 grams carbohydrate, 0 grams fat, 0 milligrams cholesterol, 1 milligram sodium

Microwave Method: Microwave cranberries and 1½ cups of the water covered in a deep 2-quart microwave-safe casserole on high 8 to 10 minutes, until berries are tender. Cool slightly and purée as directed. Mix sugar and remaining 1 cup water in a 1-quart microwave-safe measure. Microwave on high 4 to 5 minutes, until boiling. Boil 2½ to 3½ minutes, until syrupy. Proceed as directed.

♥ **LOW-CALORIE**

Grapefruit-Campari Sorbetto

Campari is an Italian bitters flavored with herbs and orange peel. You may like to try it as it is most commonly served, as an aperitif poured over ice and topped off with soda or orange juice. For a special occasion, garnish this sorbetto with pink-grapefruit sections or pomegranate seeds.

¼ **cup granulated sugar**
1½ **teaspoons unflavored gelatin**
2¼ **cups water**
1 **can (6 ounces) frozen grapefruit-juice concentrate**
¼ **cup Campari**

1. Mix sugar and gelatin in a small saucepan. Add ¼ cup of the water. Stir over low heat until sugar and gelatin are completely dissolved. Remove from heat.

2. Mix grapefruit-juice concentrate, remaining 2 cups water, the sugar mixture and Campari in a medium-size bowl.

3. Freeze in an ice-cream freezer according to manufacturer's directions. If you don't have an ice-cream freezer, pour into a 9-inch square metal pan and freeze 1 to 3 hours, until a broad rim of ice forms around the edge. Transfer to a chilled bowl and whisk or beat with an electric mixer on medium speed until smooth. Cover bowl and return to freezer. Repeat freezing and beating twice.

4. Serve as soon as frozen or freeze in an airtight container up to 1 week.

Makes 1 quart (4 cups). Per ½ cup: 64 calories, 1 gram protein, 14 grams carbohydrate, 0 grams fat, 0 milligrams cholesterol, 2 milligrams sodium

⏱ **MAKE-AHEAD**
♥ **LOW-CALORIE**

Blushing Grapefruit Granita

Unlike most frozen desserts, a granita isn't smooth and creamy but has small coarse frozen crystals. Don't make this in an ice-cream freezer; it would be too smooth.

1 **cup water**
½ **cup granulated sugar**
Peel from ½ medium-size grapefruit, removed as thinly as possible with a vegetable peeler
2 **cups fresh-squeezed grapefruit juice (from 3 medium-size grapefruits)**
1 **tablespoon grenadine (see Note)**
1 **teaspoon aromatic bitters (optional; see Note)**

1. Put water, sugar and grapefruit peel in a small saucepan. Bring to a boil over medium-high heat. Reduce heat to medium and simmer 5 minutes. Remove from heat. Let cool to room temperature. Discard peel.

2. Mix grapefruit juice, grenadine and bitters, if desired, in an 8- or 9-inch square metal pan. Stir in sugar syrup.

3. Cover with foil or plastic wrap and freeze until firm, stirring occasionally with a fork.

4. To serve: Transfer granita to refrigerator for 20 minutes to soften slightly. Serve with an ice-cream spade or scoop, or scrape surface of granita with a spoon and mound in serving dishes.

Makes 4 servings. Per serving (with bitters): 144 calories, 1 gram protein, 36 grams carbohydrate, 0 grams fat, 0 milligrams cholesterol, 2 milligrams sodium

Note: Originally made exclusively with pomegranate juice, other fruit-juice concentrates are now used to make grenadine. It adds bright red color, sweetness and a slight fruit flavor to drinks and desserts. Look for it and aromatic bitters in the cocktail-mix section of your supermarket.

Left to right: Honeydew-Melon, Plum, Mango, Grapefruit-Campari, Strawberry and Pineapple Sorbetto

Honeydew-Melon Sorbetto
(Shown on page 104)

For tips on how to choose a ripe melon, see Melons, page 23. You can make the sugar syrup up to a day ahead and leave it covered at room temperature.

- 1 large ripe honeydew melon (4 pounds), halved, seeded, rind cut off, and cut in 1-inch chunks
- 3 tablespoons fresh-squeezed lime juice
- 1 cup granulated sugar
- 1 cup water
- ¼ cup dry sherry wine or ginger ale

1. Purée melon in a food processor or a blender (you should have 4 cups purée). Pour melon purée into a large bowl. Stir in lime juice.

2. Bring sugar and water to a boil in a small heavy saucepan over medium-high heat. Boil 5 minutes. Remove from heat and let cool.

3. Stir cooled syrup and the sherry into honeydew purée.

4. Freeze in an ice-cream freezer according to manufacturer's directions. If you don't have an ice-cream freezer, pour into a 9-inch square metal pan and freeze 1 to 3 hours, until a broad rim of ice forms around the edge. Transfer to a chilled bowl and whisk or beat with an electric mixer on medium speed until smooth. Cover bowl and return to freezer. Repeat freezing and beating twice.

5. Serve as soon as frozen or freeze in an airtight container up to 1 week.

Makes about 4 cups. Per ½ cup (with sherry): 244 calories, 2 grams protein, 15 grams carbohydrate, 0 grams fat, 0 milligrams cholesterol, 9 milligrams sodium

♥ **LOW-CALORIE**
Lemon Sorbetto

This refreshing confection boasts a low calorie count.

- ¾ cup granulated sugar
- 1½ teaspoons unflavored gelatin
- ½ cup water
- 1 cup fresh-squeezed lemon juice (from 6 large lemons)

1. Mix sugar and gelatin in a small saucepan. Add water and stir over low heat until sugar and gelatin are completely dissolved. Remove from heat and stir in lemon juice.

2. Freeze in an ice-cream freezer according to manufacturer's directions. If you don't have an ice-cream freezer, pour into a 9-inch square metal pan and freeze 1 to 3 hours, until a broad rim of ice forms around the edge. Transfer to a chilled bowl and whisk or beat with an electric mixer on medium speed until smooth. Cover bowl and return to freezer. Repeat freezing and beating twice.

3. Serve as soon as frozen or freeze in an airtight container up to 1 week.

Makes 2 cups. Per ½ cup: 66 calories, 1 gram protein, 17 grams carbohydrate, 0 grams fat, 0 milligrams cholesterol, 2 milligrams sodium

♥ **LOW-CALORIE**
Lemon-Lime Ice

Only two ingredients in this easy low-calorie ice.

- 1 can (12 ounces) frozen lemon-limeade concentrate
- 2 juice-cans water

1. Mix concentrate and water until concentrate thaws and mixture has blended.

2. Freeze in an ice-cream freezer according to manufacturer's directions. If you don't have an ice-cream freezer, pour into an 8- or 9-inch metal pan. Cover and freeze 1 to 3 hours, until a broad rim of ice forms around the edge. Beat the mixture briskly with a fork to break up the ice crystals, then cover and return to freezer. Repeat freezing and beating three or four times at about 1-hour intervals. For a super-smooth ice, transfer the partially frozen mixture to a bowl and beat with an electric mixer on medium speed, then return to freezer to continue freezing.

3. Serve immediately or freeze in an airtight container up to 1 week.

Makes 4½ cups. Per ½ cup: 91 calories, 0 grams protein, 24 grams carbohydrate, 0 grams fat, 0 milligrams cholesterol, 0 milligrams sodium

Mango Sorbetto

(Shown on page 104)

3 pounds ripe mangoes, peeled
¼ cup granulated sugar
1½ teaspoons unflavored gelatin
3 tablespoons water
1 teaspoon lemon juice

1. Cut mango flesh from the pits. Scrape off any flesh clinging to pits. Purée mango in a food processor or a blender (you should have 3 cups). Scrape into a medium-size bowl.

2. Mix sugar and gelatin in a small saucepan. Add water and stir over low heat until sugar and gelatin are completely dissolved.

3. Stir gelatin mixture and lemon juice into mango purée.

4. Freeze in an ice-cream freezer according to manufacturer's directions. If you don't have an ice-cream freezer, pour into a 9-inch square metal pan and freeze 1 to 3 hours, until a broad rim of ice forms around the edge. Transfer to a chilled bowl and whisk or beat with an electric mixer on medium speed until smooth. Cover bowl and return to freezer. Repeat freezing and beating twice.

5. Serve as soon as frozen or freeze in an airtight container up to 1 week.

Makes 3 cups. Per ½ cup: 184 calories, 2 grams protein, 46 grams carbohydrate, 1 gram fat, 0 milligrams cholesterol, 17 milligrams sodium

---

♥ **LOW-CALORIE**

Mango-Lime Sorbet

(Shown on page 12)

2 large ripe mangoes, peeled
½ cup granulated sugar
3 tablespoons fresh-squeezed
   lime juice
2 tablespoons light rum or additional
   lime juice
For garnish: lime wedges

1. Cut mango flesh from the pits. Scrape off any flesh clinging to pits.

2. Put mango, sugar, lime juice and rum in a food processor or a blender and purée until smooth.

3. Freeze in an ice-cream freezer according to manufacturer's directions. If you don't have an ice-cream freezer, pour into a 9-inch metal pan and freeze 1 to 3 hours, until a broad rim of ice forms around the edge. Whisk or beat with an electric mixer on medium speed until smooth. Cover bowl and return to freezer. Repeat freezing and beating once.

4. Serve as soon as frozen or freeze in an airtight container up to 1 week. Let soften in refrigerator a few minutes before serving. Scoop or spoon into eight dessert dishes or wine glasses and garnish with lime wedges.

Makes 8 servings. Per serving (with rum): 98 calories, 0 grams protein, 23 grams carbohydrate, 0 grams fat, 0 milligrams cholesterol, 5 milligrams sodium

---

Mangoes

Mangoes are generally available all year round. They have a tough green skin that takes on a rose blush or turns red or yellow when ripe. Mangoes will usually need some ripening at home in a ripening bowl (see Melons, page 23) or at room temperature in a loosely closed paper bag. When ripe, mangoes are soft but not squishy to the touch and are fragrant at room temperature. To use, first peel the mango (the skin will pull off with the aid of a sharp knife), then cut the fruit off the oversize flat pit.

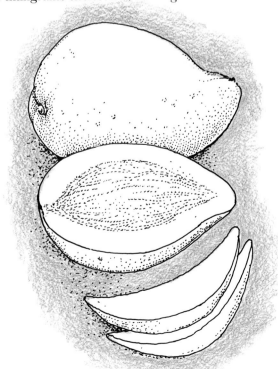

Peach Sorbet

Pineapple Sorbetto
(Shown on page 104)

If you like, top sorbetto with fresh raspberries or blueberries.

> 1 can (20 ounces) pineapple chunks in juice, well drained
> ⅓ cup granulated sugar
> 1½ teaspoons unflavored gelatin
> ⅓ cup water

1. Purée pineapple chunks in a food processor or a blender. Pour into a medium-size bowl.

2. Mix sugar and gelatin in a small saucepan. Add water and stir over low heat until sugar and gelatin are completely dissolved. Remove from heat.

3. Stir gelatin mixture into pineapple purée. Freeze in an ice-cream freezer according to manufacturer's directions. If you don't have an ice-cream freezer, pour into a 9-inch square metal pan and freeze 1 to 3 hours, until a broad rim of ice forms around the edge. Transfer to a chilled bowl and beat with a whisk or an electric mixer on medium-high speed until smooth. Cover bowl and return to freezer. Repeat freezing and beating twice.

4. Serve immediately or freeze in an airtight container up to 1 week.

Makes 2 cups. Per ½ cup: 146 calories, 1 gram protein, 37 grams carbohydrate, 0 grams fat, 0 milligrams cholesterol, 2 milligrams sodium

⏱ MAKE-AHEAD
♥ LOW-CALORIE
Peach Sorbet

> 1½ pounds ripe peaches, peeled (see Peaches, page 24), halved, pitted and cut in chunks
> ½ cup peach nectar
> 1 tablespoon granulated sugar

1. Purée peaches in a food processor or a blender.

2. Pour into an 8-inch square metal pan. Stir in peach nectar and sugar until well blended.

3. Cover and freeze about 3 hours, until firm.

4. Break up sorbet and place in food processor; process until slushy.

5. Pack in a freezer container and freeze at least 2 hours, until firm.

6. Let soften in refrigerator a few minutes before serving.

Makes 2½ cups. Per ½ cup: 56 calories, 1 gram protein, 14 grams carbohydrate, 0 grams fat, 0 milligrams cholesterol, 1 milligram sodium

Plum Sorbetto
(Shown on page 104)

The plum purée may be made ahead of time and kept at room temperature for a few hours or refrigerated overnight; let come to room temperature before proceeding.

> 2 pounds (about 12 medium-size) ripe plums, halved and pitted
> ½ cup granulated sugar
> 1 teaspoon unflavored gelatin
> 1 cup water
> ½ teaspoon almond extract

1. Put plums in a medium-size heavy saucepan (not uncoated aluminum). Cook over medium heat about 10 minutes, stirring occasionally, until soft. If needed, add 1 tablespoon water to plums as they cook to prevent scorching. Remove from heat and let cool.

2. Purée plums in a food processor or, half at a time, in a blender (you should have about 2 cups purée). There may be small bits of peel in the purée, but don't worry.

3. Mix sugar and gelatin in a small saucepan. Add water and stir over low heat until sugar and gelatin are completely dissolved. Remove from heat and stir in almond extract.

4. Stir gelatin mixture into plum purée.

5. Freeze in an ice-cream freezer according to manufacturer's directions. If you don't have an ice-cream freezer, pour into a 9-inch square metal pan and freeze 1 to 3 hours, until a broad rim of ice forms around the edge. Transfer to a chilled bowl and beat with a whisk or an electric mixer on medium speed until smooth. Cover bowl and return to freezer. Repeat freezing and beating twice.

6. Serve as soon as frozen or freeze in an airtight container up to 1 week.

Makes 2½ cups. Per ½ cup: 161 calories, 1 gram protein, 41 grams carbohydrate, 0 grams fat, 0 milligrams cholesterol, 2 milligrams sodium

Strawberry Sorbetto
(Shown on page 104)

This fresh-tasting sorbetto is one of our favorites.

> 2 pint baskets strawberries (about 7 cups), rinsed, drained and hulled
> ⅔ cup granulated sugar
> 1 cup fresh-squeezed orange juice
> ¼ cup fresh-squeezed lemon juice
> ¼ cup Grand Marnier or other orange-flavor liqueur, or an additional ¼ cup orange juice

1. Blot strawberries dry with paper towels. Place in a medium-size bowl and mash with a pastry blender or a potato masher. Sprinkle with ⅓ cup of the sugar. Let stand at room temperature 30 minutes, tossing often.

2. Mix remaining ⅓ cup sugar and the orange and lemon juices in a small heavy saucepan. Stir over low heat until sugar dissolves. Remove from heat and let cool.

3. Purée mashed berries in a food processor or a blender. Be sure any sugar that sinks to the bottom of the blender is mixed in.

4. Return puréed berries to bowl. Stir in juice mixture and liqueur.

5. Freeze in an ice-cream freezer according to manufacturer's directions. If you don't have an ice-cream freezer, pour into a 9-inch square metal pan and freeze 1 to 3 hours, until a broad rim of ice forms around the edge. Transfer to a chilled bowl and beat with a whisk or an electric mixer on medium speed until smooth. Cover bowl and return to freezer. Repeat freezing and beating twice.

6. Serve as soon as frozen or freeze in an airtight container up to 1 week.

Makes 1 quart (4 cups). Per ½ cup (with Grand Marnier): 113 calories, 1 gram protein, 27 grams carbohydrate, 0 grams fat, 0 milligrams cholesterol, 2 milligrams sodium

Tangerine Ice in Orange Shells

Tangerine Ice in Orange Shells

This popular way of serving citrus ices looks fancy and can be made ahead.

2 **cans (6 ounces each) frozen tangerine-juice or orange-juice concentrate**
3 **juice-cans water**
1 **envelope unflavored gelatin**
½ **cup granulated sugar**
6 **large navel oranges**
For garnish: fresh mint and strawberries

1. Stir tangerine-juice concentrate and water in a medium-size bowl until concentrate thaws. Pour ½ cup of the mixture into a small saucepan (not uncoated aluminum). Sprinkle with gelatin and let stand 1 minute.

2. Place saucepan over low heat and stir with a rubber or plastic spatula until gelatin is completely dissolved and mixture is almost boiling. Remove from heat.

3. Stir gelatin mixture into remaining juice mixture. Add sugar and stir until dissolved.

4. Freeze in an ice-cream freezer according to manufacturer's directions. If you don't have an ice-cream freezer, pour into a shallow 9-inch square metal pan. Cover and freeze 1 to 3 hours, until a broad rim of ice forms around the edge. Beat mixture briskly with a fork to break up ice crystals, then cover and return to freezer. Repeat

freezing and beating three or four times at 45- to 60-minute intervals until mixture is slightly mushy.

5. Meanwhile, using a small knife, slice off about one third of each orange. Scoop out pulp from larger pieces with a spoon or a melon baller. Cut a sawtooth design in edge of shells with a small sharp knife or scissors.

6. Fill shells with tangerine ice and serve, or wrap filled shells in an airtight container and freeze up to 1 week.

7. Just before serving, garnish with mint and strawberries.

Makes 6 servings. Per serving: 182 calories, 2 grams protein, 44 grams carbohydrate, 1 gram fat, 0 milligrams cholesterol, 3 milligrams sodium

Watermelon-Mint Ice

A summer favorite. The sugar syrup may be made a few hours ahead, strained and kept at room temperature.

½ **cup granulated sugar**
½ **cup water**
20 **fresh mint leaves**
6 **cups peeled, seeded watermelon chunks (from 4 to 5 pounds watermelon)**

1. Stir sugar, water and mint in a small saucepan over low heat until sugar dissolves. Raise heat to medium, stop stirring; bring to a boil. Boil 3 minutes. Remove from heat; let cool.

2. Pour syrup though a strainer suspended over a medium-size bowl. Discard mint.

3. Purée melon in a food processor or a blender until smooth (you should have 4 cups purée). Add to sugar syrup and stir to mix well.

4. Freeze in an ice-cream freezer according to manufacturer's directions. If you don't have an ice-cream freezer, pour into a 9-inch square metal pan and freeze 1 to 3 hours, until a broad rim of ice forms around the edge. Then beat with a fork to break up ice crystals; cover and freeze. Repeat freezing and beating three times at 1-hour intervals.

5. Serve immediately or freeze in an airtight container up to 1 week.

Makes 4½ cups. Per ½ cup: 71 calories, 1 gram protein, 18 grams carbohydrate, 0 grams fat, 0 milligrams cholesterol, 1 milligram sodium

Citrus Sherbet Mold

You can make this mold with any flavor sherbet or sorbet and fill the center with any combination of berries or sliced fruit. While sorbets are not as creamy as sherbets, they have a fruitier flavor and fewer calories.

---

2 pints orange sherbet or sorbet
1 pint lemon sherbet or sorbet
About 3 cups fresh raspberries
For garnish: fresh mint

1. Place a 6-cup fluted tube pan in freezer to chill.

2. Meanwhile, put sherbet in refrigerator for 10 to 15 minutes, until soft but not melted around the edges.

3. Scoop 1 pint of orange sherbet into bottom of chilled pan. Press into a firm, even layer with a rubber spatula. Top with lemon sherbet, then the remaining pint of orange, pressing each layer firmly. Cover pan with plastic wrap.

4. Freeze overnight or up to 1 week.

5. To unmold: Dip pan into enough cold water to reach ¾ up side of pan for 30 to 60 seconds, just until sherbet starts to loosen from sides. Wipe pan and unmold onto serving plate. Return to freezer for 1 to 2 hours.

6. To serve: Fill center with raspberries and garnish with mint.

Makes 12 servings. Per serving (made with sherbet): 128 calories, 1 gram protein, 29 grams carbohydrate, 1 gram fat, 7 milligrams cholesterol, 40 milligrams sodium

Citrus Sherbet Mold

Sauces

Turn a dish of fruit, a bowl of berries or a scoop of ice cream into a scene-stealing dessert with these surprisingly simple sauces.

Clockwise from top right: Blueberry-Lemon Sauce, Rum Bananas, Glazed Brandied Pears

Fruit Sauces

⏰ MAKE-AHEAD

Apricot Sauce

Spoon over peach ice cream and garnish with sliced fresh peaches, or pour over banana ice cream and top with toasted walnuts.

---

1 can (8¾ ounces) unpeeled apricot
    halves in heavy syrup, undrained
3 tablespoons granulated sugar
¼ cup orange juice

---

1. Put apricots and their syrup, sugar and orange juice in a food processor or a blender and process until smooth.

2. Pour purée into a small heavy saucepan and bring to a boil over high heat, stirring constantly. Reduce heat to medium and simmer sauce 7 minutes, checking often so that sauce doesn't boil over or burn.

3. Serve sauce hot or cover and refrigerate up to 1 month and serve chilled or warm. To reheat, see Reheating Sauces, page 121.

Makes 1 cup. Per 2 tablespoons: 47 calories, 0 grams protein, 12 grams carbohydrate, 0 grams fat, 0 milligrams cholesterol, 0 milligrams sodium

---

✳ MICROWAVE

Rum Bananas

(Shown on page 112)

Serve over vanilla ice cream. For a nice crunch, sprinkle toasted pecans on top.

½ cup packed light-brown sugar
¼ cup light rum
¼ cup butter or margarine
2 large bananas, halved crosswise,
    then lengthwise

---

1. Mix sugar and rum in a 9-inch microwave-safe glass pie plate. Microwave uncovered on high 2 minutes, until sugar is dissolved.

2. Stir in butter and microwave 2 to 3 minutes longer until sauce thickens.

3. Add bananas and turn to coat. Microwave on high 30 to 60 seconds to heat bananas.

4. Let stand 5 minutes before serving.

Makes 4 servings. Per serving: 271 calories, 1 gram protein, 40 grams carbohydrate, 12 grams fat, 36 milligrams cholesterol with butter, 0 milligrams cholesterol with margarine, 149 milligrams sodium

---

⏰ MAKE-AHEAD
✳ MICROWAVE

Blueberry-Lemon Sauce

(Shown on page 112)

Spoon this sauce over ice cream, cheesecake, crepes or shortcake or, as shown here, fresh melon balls.

½ cup granulated sugar
1 tablespoon cornstarch
1 pint basket blueberries, rinsed and
    drained (about 3 cups), or 3 cups
    thawed unsweetened frozen
    blueberries
1 teaspoon lemon juice

---

1. Mix sugar and cornstarch in a 2-quart microwave-safe bowl. Stir in 2 cups of the blueberries and the lemon juice.

2. Cover with a lid or vented plastic wrap and microwave on high 5 to 6 minutes, stirring twice, until mixture comes to a boil.

3. Stir in remaining 1 cup berries and let cool.

4. Serve at room temperature or cover and chill until ready to serve.

Makes 2¼ cups. Per ¼ cup: 76 calories, 0 grams protein, 19 grams carbohydrate, 0 grams fat, 0 milligrams cholesterol, 1 milligram sodium

---

⏰ MAKE-AHEAD

Double Blueberry Sauce

Serve warm or chilled over vanilla, strawberry or raspberry ice cream. Terrific as a pound-cake, pancake or waffle topping, too.

---

1 pint basket blueberries, rinsed and
    drained (about 3 cups)
⅓ cup granulated sugar
2 tablespoons water
1 teaspoon vanilla extract

---

1. Put 2 cups of the blueberries, the sugar and water in a medium-size saucepan (not uncoated aluminum). Bring to a boil over medium heat. Simmer 10 to 15 minutes, stirring occasionally, until sauce thickens. Remove from heat.

2. Let sauce stand until warm. Stir in remaining 1 cup blueberries and the vanilla.

3. Serve warm or cover and chill until ready to serve.

Makes 2 cups. Per ¼ cup: 66 calories, 0 grams protein, 17 grams carbohydrate, 0 grams fat, 0 milligrams cholesterol, 1 milligram sodium

Blueberry-Ginger Sauce

Serve over pancakes, ice cream or plain cakes. The sauce may be refrigerated up to four weeks.

- **1 cup apple juice**
- **1 cup granulated sugar**
- **1 tablespoon cornstarch**
- **1 teaspoon ground ginger**
- **1 cinnamon stick (about 2½ inches long)**
- **2 bags (12 ounces each) frozen blueberries**

1. Heat juice, sugar, cornstarch and ginger in a medium-size saucepan (not uncoated aluminum) over high heat. Stir until sugar dissolves. Add cinnamon stick and bring mixture to a boil.

2. Immediately add frozen blueberries. Reduce heat to medium and cook 12 to 15 minutes, stirring three or four times, just until mixture boils, some berries burst and liquid thickens to the consistency of maple syrup. Remove from heat. Discard cinnamon stick.

3. Pour into clean hot glass jars. Cover tightly. Let cool. Refrigerate until ready to serve.

Makes 4 cups. Per ¼ cup: 84 calories, 0 grams protein, 21 grams carbohydrate, 0 grams fat, 0 milligrams cholesterol, 1 milligram sodium

Cantaloupe Sauce

This bright orange sauce makes a lovely presentation over cut-up honeydew melon. It's fine over other fruits and with ice cream, too.

- **1 cantaloupe (about 1¼ pounds), halved, seeded, rind cut off, and cut in chunks (about 3 cups)**
- **2 tablespoons honey, or to taste**
- **2 teaspoons grated fresh orange peel**

1. Put all ingredients in a food processor or a blender and process to a slightly chunky sauce.

2. Scrape into a medium-size bowl.

3. Serve immediately or cover and chill until ready to serve.

Makes 2 cups. Per ¼ cup: 36 calories, 0 grams protein, 9 grams carbohydrate, 0 grams fat, 0 milligrams cholesterol, 7 milligrams sodium

Blueberries with Honey and Lime, Double Blueberry Sauce

Brandied Cranberry-Apple Sauce

This ice-cream topping is equally delicious without the brandy. It can be made ahead and reheated before serving. Spoon over cinnamon or vanilla ice cream.

    4 large Granny Smith apples (about
        2 pounds), peeled, cored and
        thinly sliced
    ½ cup apple juice
    1 bag (12 ounces) fresh or frozen
        cranberries
    ⅔ cup packed brown sugar
    ½ cup raisins
    ½ cup chopped walnuts
 1¼ teaspoons ground cinnamon
    ¼ teaspoon ground ginger
    ⅛ teaspoon ground nutmeg
    ¼ cup brandy

1. Bring apples and apple juice to a boil in a large saucepan (not uncoated aluminum) over medium-high heat. Reduce heat to low, cover and simmer 8 minutes. Apples will be crisp-tender.

2. Stir in cranberries, sugar, raisins, walnuts, cinnamon, ginger and nutmeg. Cover and cook over medium heat about 10 minutes, stirring twice, until cranberries pop and apples are tender.

3. Just before serving, spoon apple mixture into a flameproof serving bowl. Warm brandy in a small saucepan over low heat. Pour over the apple mixture and carefully ignite with a long wooden match or taper. When flames die, serve.

Makes 8 servings. Per ½ cup: 234 calories, 1 gram protein, 50 grams carbohydrate, 5 grams fat, 0 milligrams cholesterol, 24 milligrams sodium

Lemon Dessert Sauce

(Shown on page 124)

To extract more juice, microwave the lemons on high for 30 seconds before squeezing. Serve sauce warm over berries or sliced ripe fruit.

    ½ cup butter or margarine
    1 cup granulated sugar
    1 teaspoon finely grated fresh
        lemon peel
    ⅓ cup fresh-squeezed lemon juice
    ¼ cup thawed frozen cholesterol-free
        egg product

1. Put butter in a 4-cup microwave-safe glass measure or a deep bowl. Microwave butter on high 45 to 60 seconds, until melted. Whisk in sugar, lemon peel and juice, then the egg product until thoroughly blended.

2. Microwave on medium-high 2 to 3 minutes, stirring twice, until sugar is dissolved and sauce is slightly thickened.

3. Serve sauce warm.

Makes 1⅔ cups. Per 2 tablespoons: 130 calories, 1 gram protein, 16 grams carbohydrate, 8 grams fat, 41 milligrams cholesterol with butter, 0 milligrams cholesterol with margarine, 91 milligrams sodium

Lemon-Mint Sauce

This refreshing clear sauce is lovely over blueberries or peeled fresh Bartlett pears, or tossed with a mixture of cut-up ripe summer fruits.

    1 cup light corn syrup
    1 cup loosely packed fresh mint leaves
    ¼ cup fresh-squeezed lemon juice
    1 tablespoon grated fresh lemon peel

1. Mix corn syrup, mint leaves and lemon juice in a small heavy saucepan. Bring to a simmer over low heat; simmer 5 minutes. Remove from heat.

2. Strain through a fine strainer suspended over a small bowl, pressing on the mint to extract all the liquid; discard mint. Stir in lemon peel.

3. Cover and chill until ready to serve.

Makes 1⅓ cups. Per ⅓ cup: 194 calories, 0 grams protein, 50 grams carbohydrate, 0 grams fat, 0 milligrams cholesterol, 45 milligrams sodium

Orange Cream Sauce

The acid in the juice thickens the cream. This is especially luscious over mixed fresh summer fruits, but it also goes well with plain berries, peaches, plums, pears or nectarines.

¾ cup heavy cream
2 tablespoons partially thawed frozen
orange-juice concentrate
1 tablespoon granulated sugar

1. Stir heavy cream, orange-juice concentrate and sugar in a small bowl until well blended.

2. Cover and chill about 30 minutes, until sauce is thickened, before serving.

Makes 1 cup. Per ¼ cup: 183 calories, 1 gram protein, 8 grams carbohydrate, 17 grams fat, 59 milligrams cholesterol, 14 milligrams sodium

⏱ MAKE-AHEAD
Peach-Citrus Conserve

This is a delicious topping for ice cream as well as a spread for toast. It keeps well in the refrigerator up to three weeks.

4 cans (16 ounces each) sliced cling
peaches packed in juice or extra-
light syrup, drained
1 cup granulated sugar
¼ cup fresh-squeezed lemon juice
⅓ cup sweet orange marmalade
1 teaspoon grated fresh gingerroot or
½ teaspoon ground ginger

1. Coarsely chop peaches in a food processor or a blender.

2. Mix peaches with sugar and lemon juice in a medium-size heavy saucepan (not uncoated aluminum). Bring to a boil over medium-high heat. Reduce heat to medium-low. Simmer 30 minutes, stirring often to prevent scorching.

3. Stir marmalade and gingerroot into peaches. Simmer 10 minutes longer, until conserve is thick and liquid looks clear.

4. Pour into clean hot jars and cover tightly with jar lids. Let cool before refrigerating up to 3 weeks.

Makes 5 cups. Per tablespoon: 23 calories, 0 grams protein, 6 grams carbohydrate, 0 grams fat, 0 milligrams cholesterol, 1 milligram sodium

⏱ MAKE-AHEAD
Peach-Almond Sauce

Grown-ups usually like this flavor better than children do. Good on pound cake, ice cream or frozen yogurt, and it makes an interesting change from syrup when spooned over waffles or pancakes.

⅓ cup granulated sugar
½ cup water
¼ cup almond-flavor liqueur or ½
teaspoon almond extract
1 cup thinly sliced fresh peaches

1. Bring sugar and water to a boil in a small saucepan over medium-high heat. Reduce heat to low and simmer 5 minutes. Remove from heat and stir in liqueur.

2. Put peaches in a small bowl. Pour hot syrup over peaches. Cover and let stand at room temperature 1 hour.

3. Serve immediately or cover and refrigerate until ready to serve.

Makes 1½ cups. Per ¼ cup (with liqueur): 90 calories, 0 grams protein, 20 grams carbohydrate, 0 grams fat, 0 milligrams cholesterol, 1 milligram sodium

Orange Cream Sauce

Quick Raspberry Sauce

The rich red color and pure fruit taste complement all berries as well as cantaloupe and honeydew melon. This is also a good topping for ice cream, and it couldn't be easier to prepare: There's only one ingredient.

1 package (10 ounces) thawed frozen raspberries in syrup

1. Purée berries in a food processor or a blender. Strain through a fine strainer suspended over a small bowl to remove seeds; discard seeds.

2. Serve immediately or cover and chill until ready to serve.

Makes 1 cup. Per ¼ cup: 70 calories, 1 gram protein, 17 grams carbohydrate, 0 grams fat, 0 milligrams cholesterol, 1 milligram sodium

Rhubarb Sauce

Serve over strawberry ice cream and top with sliced strawberries, or spoon on vanilla ice cream and sprinkle with cold fresh blueberries.

⅔ cup granulated sugar
1 tablespoon cornstarch
½ teaspoon grated fresh lemon peel
¼ teaspoon ground cinnamon
1½ cups water
2 cups coarsely chopped fresh or thawed frozen rhubarb
2 tablespoons fresh-squeezed lemon juice

1. Mix sugar, cornstarch, lemon peel, cinnamon and water in a medium-size saucepan (not uncoated aluminum). Stir over low heat until sugar dissolves.

2. Add rhubarb to saucepan and bring to a boil. Reduce heat to low and simmer about 5 minutes, stirring occasionally, until rhubarb is tender and sauce has thickened and cleared. Remove from heat; stir in lemon juice. Pour into a bowl.

3. Cover sauce and chill. Serve cold. Refrigerate up to 2 weeks.

Makes 3 cups. Per ¼ cup: 48 calories, 0 grams protein, 12 grams carbohydrate, 0 grams fat, 0 milligrams cholesterol, 1 milligram sodium

Quick Strawberry Sauce

This sauce couldn't be simpler, and it's a good way to use up less-than-perfect berries. Adjust the sugar and lemon juice to your taste. Serve over plain cake or ice cream.

1 pint basket strawberries, rinsed, drained and hulled (about 3 cups)
½ cup granulated sugar
2 tablespoons lemon juice

1. Put all ingredients in a blender or a food processor and process until smooth. Pour into a small bowl.

2. Cover sauce and refrigerate up to 2 days until ready to use.

Makes about 1⅔ cups. Per 2 tablespoons: 39 calories, 0 grams protein, 21 grams carbohydrate, 0 grams fat, 0 milligrams cholesterol, 0 milligrams sodium

Strawberry-Patch Sauce

For a festive occasion, try Grand Marnier or another orange-flavor liqueur instead of the orange juice. Make the sauce a few hours before serving so that the flavor can develop. Serve over fudge-swirl ice cream topped with sliced fresh strawberries. Try pouring it over pralines-and-cream ice cream, then topping with toasted pecans.

1 pint basket strawberries, rinsed, drained and hulled (about 3 cups)
¾ cup granulated sugar
½ cup red-currant jelly
¼ cup orange juice

1. Process strawberries and sugar in a food processor or a blender until smooth and sugar is dissolved.

2. Mix jelly and juice in a small saucepan and stir over low heat until jelly dissolves. Add to berry mixture; process just to blend. Pour into a bowl.

3. Cover sauce and chill. Refrigerate up to 3 days or freeze up to 2 weeks.

Makes 3 cups. Per ¼ cup: 98 calories, 0 grams protein, 25 grams carbohydrate, 0 grams fat, 0 milligrams cholesterol, 3 milligrams sodium

(Clockwise from left) Quick Strawberry Sauce (shown over ice cream), Chocolate-Mint Sauce (shown over pears), and Quick Raspberry Sauce (shown over honeydew melon)

Chocolate Sauces

🕐 MAKE-AHEAD

No-Fudging Hot Fudge Sauce

Good on chocolate ice cream topped with whipped cream and decorated with chocolate curls. Or spoon sauce over butter-almond ice cream and sprinkle with whole almonds.

    4 squares (1 ounce each)
        unsweetened chocolate
    3 tablespoons butter or margarine
    ⅔ cup boiling water
    1⅔ cups granulated sugar
    6 tablespoons light corn syrup

1. Stir chocolate and butter in a medium-size heavy saucepan over low heat until melted and smooth.

2. Add boiling water and stir until blended. Stir in sugar and corn syrup. Raise heat to medium-high and stir until mixture starts to boil. Reduce heat to low and simmer 9 minutes, until slightly reduced and thickened.

3. Serve hot or cover and refrigerate up to 1 month. To reheat, see Reheating Sauces, on page 121.

Makes 2¾ cups. Per 2 tablespoons: 114 calories, 1 gram protein, 21 grams carbohydrate, 4 grams fat, 5 milligrams cholesterol with butter, 0 milligrams cholesterol with margarine, 23 milligrams sodium

🕐 MAKE-AHEAD

Chocolate-Rum-Almond Sauce

Delicious served warm over ice cream. Keeps up to one month in the refrigerator.

    ⅔ cup half-and-half
    ¼ cup granulated sugar
    8 ounces semisweet chocolate chips
        (1⅓ cups)
    1 tablespoon butter or margarine
    1 cup chopped blanched almonds
    ½ teaspoon rum flavoring

1. Stir half-and-half and sugar in a medium-size heavy saucepan over low heat until sugar dissolves. Add chocolate and stir until it is melted and mixture is smooth. Remove from heat.

2. Stir butter into chocolate mixture until melted. Stir in almonds and rum flavoring.

3. Serve warm or pour into a glass jar. Cover tightly and refrigerate up to 1 month until ready to serve. To reheat, see Reheating Sauces on page 121.

Makes 2 cups. Per 2 tablespoons: 152 calories, 2 grams protein, 13 grams carbohydrate, 11 grams fat, 7 milligrams cholesterol with butter, 5 milligrams cholesterol with margarine, 14 milligrams sodium

No-Fudging Hot Fudge Sauce

Brittle Chocolate-Walnut Sauce

Spoon hot sauce over ice cream; it will harden immediately. Store leftover sauce tightly covered in the refrigerator. Reheat over low heat.

¼ cup butter or margarine
½ cup chopped walnuts
4 squares (1 ounce each) semisweet
    chocolate, broken up

1. Melt butter in a small heavy saucepan over medium heat. Add walnuts and cook about 5 minutes, stirring often, until lightly browned.

2. Reduce heat to low. Add chocolate and stir constantly until melted. Remove from heat.

3. Serve immediately or cover and chill up to 3 weeks or until ready to serve.

Makes 1 cup. Per tablespoon: 86 calories, 1 gram protein, 5 grams carbohydrate, 8 grams fat, 9 milligrams cholesterol with butter, 0 milligrams cholesterol with margarine, 35 milligrams sodium

Chocolate-Mint Sauce
(Shown on page 119)

Delicious over drained canned pear halves or frozen coffee yogurt.

12 thin dark-chocolate-covered mints
    (about 6 ounces)
⅓ cup heavy cream

1. Heat mints and cream in a small heavy saucepan over low heat about 3 minutes, stirring constantly, until mints are melted and sauce is smooth.

2. Serve immediately.

Makes ⅔ cup. Per tablespoon: 88 calories, 0 grams protein, 13 grams carbohydrate, 4 grams fat, 10 milligrams cholesterol, 31 milligrams sodium

Shiny Chocolate Sauce or Glaze

Makes a perfect shiny glaze for cake or a rich sauce over ice cream.

1 package (6 ounces) semisweet
    chocolate chips (1 cup)
⅓ cup heavy cream

1. Put chocolate chips in a small heavy saucepan and melt over low heat, stirring occasionally, until smooth. Remove from heat and stir in heavy cream until well blended.

2. Serve immediately or cover and chill until ready to use. To reheat, see Reheating Sauces below.

Makes about 1 cup. Per tablespoon: 71 calories, 1 gram protein, 6 grams carbohydrate, 6 grams fat, 7 milligrams cholesterol, 2 milligrams sodium

---

Reheating Sauces

☐ **ON RANGE TOP:** Spoon into a small heavy saucepan and stir constantly over low heat until warm or hot. Or remove lid and place jar in a saucepan of simmering water, stirring occasionally, until warm or hot.

☐ **IN MICROWAVE:** Remove lid if sauce is in a glass jar, or transfer to a microwave-safe container. Cover loosely with waxed paper. Microwave on high 1 minute; stir, then repeat in 30-second intervals, stirring after each, until sauce reaches the desired temperature.

Sauces with Nuts

⏱ MAKE-AHEAD

Peanut-Vanilla Sauce

Serve sauce spooned over strawberry ice cream topped with banana slices, or ladle over banana ice cream and sprinkle with crushed peanut brittle. This sauce keeps in the refrigerator up to two weeks.

¾ cup light corn syrup
2 tablespoons water
⅓ cup smooth peanut butter
1 tablespoon butter or margarine
½ cup heavy cream
1 teaspoon vanilla extract

1. Mix corn syrup and water in a small heavy saucepan. Bring to a boil over medium heat. Reduce heat to low and simmer 6 minutes, until syrupy. Whisk in peanut butter. Don't worry if the sauce looks curdled; it will smooth out later. Remove from heat.

2. Add butter and stir until melted. Stir in cream and vanilla. Pour into a small bowl. Cover and chill until ready to serve.

3. Serve cold.

Makes 1½ cups. Per 2 tablespoons: 133 calories, 2 grams protein, 17 grams carbohydrate, 7 grams fat, 12 milligrams cholesterol with butter, 3 milligrams cholesterol with margarine, 71 milligrams sodium

⏱ MAKE-AHEAD
✳ MICROWAVE

Southern-Praline Ice-Cream Sauce

This sauce is good over sliced pears or plain cake. It makes a lovely holiday-time gift.

1¼ cups coarsely chopped pecans
7 tablespoons butter or margarine
1¼ cups packed light-brown sugar
3 tablespoons all-purpose flour
¾ cup light corn syrup
1 can (5 ounces, about ⅔ cup)
   evaporated milk

1. Put pecans and 3 tablespoons of the butter in an 11x7-inch microwave-safe baking dish. Microwave on high 8 to 10 minutes, stirring twice, until pecans are light golden brown.

Maple-Nut Sauce

2. Put remaining 4 tablespoons butter in a 4-cup microwave-safe measure or a deep bowl. Microwave on high 45 to 60 seconds, until butter melts.

3. Whisk sugar and flour into butter. Then whisk in corn syrup until thoroughly blended.

4. Microwave on high 6 to 8 minutes, stirring twice, until sugar is dissolved and sauce is thickened. Let stand 2 minutes.

5. Carefully stir in milk and pecans with a long-handled wooden spoon. Let cool slightly.

6. Pour into clean hot jars or containers. Cover tightly and cool before refrigerating. To reheat, see Reheating Sauces, page 121.

Makes 3 cups. Per 2 tablespoons: 157 calories, 1 gram protein, 21 grams carbohydrate, 8 grams fat, 13 milligrams cholesterol with butter, 4 milligrams cholesterol with margarine, 60 milligrams sodium

⏱ MAKE-AHEAD

Maple-Nut Sauce

Serve this over coffee or butter-pecan ice cream and sprinkle with chocolate "coffee" beans.

1½ cups coarsely chopped walnuts
   or pecans
1 cup pure maple syrup
3 tablespoons butter or margarine
⅓ cup heavy cream
½ teaspoon vanilla extract

1. Heat oven to 350°F. Spread nuts on a baking sheet and bake 10 to 15 minutes, until toasted and golden brown (or toast in your microwave oven; see Microwave Tips for Desserts, page 33). Remove from heat and let cool on a wire rack.

2. Bring maple syrup to a boil in a medium-size saucepan over high heat. Boil until it reaches the soft-ball stage, 234°F on a candy thermometer or when syrup forms a soft ball when dropped into very cold water and flattens when removed from water. Remove saucepan from heat. Add butter and stir until melted.

3. Pour syrup into a medium-size bowl and let cool 5 minutes. Add nuts, cream and vanilla to syrup and stir to blend.

4. Serve immediately or cover and chill to serve cold. Refrigerate up to 2 weeks. To reheat, see Reheating Sauces, page 121.

Makes 1¾ cups. Per 2 tablespoons: 185 calories, 1 gram protein, 17 grams carbohydrate, 14 grams fat, 15 milligrams cholesterol with butter, 7 milligrams cholesterol with margarine, 34 milligrams sodium

Creamy Sauces

★ SPECIAL—AND WORTH IT
Best-Ever Butterscotch Sauce

Fantastic flavor but a little tricky to make. The caramelized sugar is extremely hot, about 400°F, so be careful. If you like, add 3 tablespoons bourbon to the sauce with the butter. Wonderful spooned over French-vanilla ice cream topped with crumbled English toffee candy. Or try spooning it over peach ice cream and topping the sundae with sliced peaches.

- **1 cup granulated sugar**
- **⅓ cup water**
- **1 cup heavy cream**
- **3 tablespoons butter or margarine**
- **1 teaspoon vanilla extract**

1. Mix sugar and water in a medium-size heavy saucepan. Heat over low heat, stirring occasionally, until sugar dissolves, about 15 minutes.

2. Raise heat to high and bring syrup to a boil. While cooking, wash down the sides of the pan with a wet pastry brush to make sure all sugar dissolves. Boil about 10 minutes without stirring, until syrup is a deep rich caramel color. If syrup begins to color in one section of the pan first, gently rotate the pan to swirl the darkening part into the rest (don't stir). Remove from heat.

3. Meanwhile, heat cream in a small saucepan over medium heat just until bubbles form around the edges. Remove from heat.

4. Stirring syrup constantly, slowly add cream. (Be careful. Mixture will froth and bubble vigorously and climb up sides of pan.) Add butter and vanilla and stir until smooth.

5. Serve syrup hot or cold. Refrigerate up to 1 week. To reheat, see Reheating Sauces, page 121.

Makes 1½ cups. Per 2 tablespoons: 159 calories, 0 grams protein, 17 grams carbohydrate, 10 grams fat, 35 milligrams cholesterol with butter, 26 milligrams cholesterol with margarine, 42 milligrams sodium

Clockwise from right: Lemon Dessert Sauce (shown over strawberries); Caramel Sauce (shown over cake); Rum Sauce (shown over ice cream)

Caramel Sauce

Wonderful spooned over pound cake, coffee ice cream or frozen yogurt.

- ¼ **cup butter or margarine**
- 1 **cup packed brown sugar**
- ½ **cup heavy cream**

1. Put butter in a 4-cup glass measure or a deep microwave-safe bowl. Microwave on high 45 to 60 seconds, until melted. Whisk in sugar and cream until smooth.

2. Microwave on high 2 to 2½ minutes, stirring once, until sauce is bubbly and slightly thickened.

3. Serve warm.

Makes 1½ cups. Per 2 tablespoons: 137 calories, 0 grams protein, 18 grams carbohydrate, 8 grams fat, 25 milligrams cholesterol with butter, 3 milligrams cholesterol with margarine, 55 milligrams sodium

---

🕐 **MAKE-AHEAD**

Creamy Citrus Sauce

When you're pressed for time and a crowd is coming for dessert, whip up this sauce to spoon over slices of store-bought pound cake or angel-food cake. Top with sliced fresh strawberries or, if nice berries aren't available, thawed frozen strawberries in syrup.

- ¾ **cup granulated sugar**
- 3 **tablespoons cornstarch**
- 2 **teaspoons grated fresh orange peel**
- ½ **teaspoon grated fresh lemon peel**
- ⅓ **cup fresh-squeezed orange juice**
- 2 **tablespoons fresh-squeezed lemon juice**
- **Yolk from 1 large egg**
- 1 **tablespoon butter or margarine**
- **Pinch of salt (optional)**
- 1 **cup boiling water**
- 1 **cup heavy cream**

1. Mix sugar and water in a heavy medium-size saucepan (not uncoated aluminum). Whisk in citrus peels and juices and the egg yolk. Stir in the butter and salt, if desired. Gradually stir in the boiling water until blended.

2. Place saucepan over medium heat and bring to a simmer, stirring often. Cook 5 minutes, stirring often, until sauce is thickened. Remove from heat and refrigerate uncovered until chilled.

3. Beat cream with an electric mixer on high speed until soft peaks form when beaters are lifted. Fold cream into chilled sauce mixture and serve.

Makes 3½ cups. Per ¼ cup: 120 calories, 0 grams protein, 14 grams carbohydrate, 7 grams fat, 25 milligrams cholesterol with butter, 22 milligrams cholesterol with margarine, 16 milligrams sodium

---

🕐 **MAKE-AHEAD**

Buttermilk-Spice Sauce

The slight tang of the buttermilk enhances the flavors of sweet ripe peaches, nectarines, cantaloupe, honeydew melon and especially blueberries.

- ½ **cup buttermilk**
- ½ **cup sour cream**
- 1 **tablespoon granulated sugar**
- ⅓ **teaspoon ground cardamom or ginger**

1. Mix buttermilk, sour cream, sugar and cardamom in a small bowl until well blended and smooth.

2. Cover and chill until ready to serve.

Makes 1 cup. Per ¼ cup: 84 calories, 2 grams protein, 6 grams carbohydrate, 6 grams fat, 13 milligrams cholesterol, 55 milligrams sodium

---

🕐 **MAKE-AHEAD**

Honey-Cream Sauce

Equally good served warm or cold, this sweet sauce is a fine choice to top fruits that aren't at their peak.

- ½ **cup honey**
- ½ **cup half-and-half**
- 2 **tablespoons butter or margarine**

1. Mix honey, half-and-half and butter in a small heavy saucepan. Bring to a boil over medium-high heat. Reduce heat to low and simmer 10 minutes, stirring occasionally, until sauce is slightly thickened.

2. Serve warm or cover and chill until ready to serve.

Makes 1 cup. Per ¼ cup: 220 calories, 1 gram protein, 36 grams carbohydrate, 9 grams fat, 31 milligrams cholesterol with butter, 13 milligrams cholesterol with margarine, 86 milligrams sodium

Spirited Sauces

⊙ MAKE-AHEAD
✳ MICROWAVE
Bourbon Sauce

Refrigerate leftover sauce in a microwave-safe container. Reheat on defrost or medium setting to warm. Sauce is good over pound cake or fruit cake or ice cream.

---

6 tablespoons butter or margarine
½ cup granulated sugar
¼ cup thawed cholesterol-free
    egg product
3 tablespoons bourbon

1. Put butter in a 4-cup glass measure or a deep microwave-safe bowl. Microwave on high 30 to 45 seconds, until melted. Stir in sugar and egg product until blended.

2. Microwave on medium 2 to 3 minutes, stirring once, until sauce thickens slightly.

3. Let sauce cool about 3 minutes, then stir in bourbon.

4. Serve warm.

Makes about 1 cup. Per 2 tablespoons: 127 calories, 1 gram protein, 13 grams carbohydrate, 9 grams fat, 23 milligrams cholesterol with butter, 0 milligrams cholesterol with margarine, 98 milligrams sodium

⊙ MAKE-AHEAD
Brandied Brown-Sugar Sauce

Our tasters loved this sauce spooned over a mixture of sliced ripe peaches and fresh raspberries, but it's good over sliced bananas, fresh pineapple and seedless grapes, too. You can top it off with a dollop of sour cream or plain yogurt.

¼ cup butter or margarine
⅔ cup packed light-brown sugar
¼ cup brandy (see Note)
¼ cup water

1. Melt butter in a small skillet over medium heat until bubbly. Add brown sugar, brandy and water. Bring to a simmer.

2. Simmer 2 to 3 minutes, stirring constantly, until sugar dissolves and sauce thickens.

3. Serve immediately over fruit or cover and chill. Reheat over low heat before serving.

Makes 1 cup. Per ¼ cup: 237 calories, 0 grams protein, 35 grams carbohydrate, 11 grams fat, 36 milligrams cholesterol with butter, 0 milligrams cholesterol with margarine, 151 milligrams sodium

Note: You can omit the brandy and use ½ cup water plus 1 teaspoon brandy flavoring, but the sauce will be thinner since the brandy evaporates during cooking.

✳ MICROWAVE
Rum Sauce
(Shown on page 124)

You can omit the rum if you like, substituting either 1 tablespoon rum flavoring or 1 teaspoon light molasses. Serve over ice cream or plain cake.

---

6 tablespoons butter or margarine
½ cup granulated sugar
¼ cup thawed frozen cholesterol-free
    egg product
2 to 3 tablespoons dark rum

1. Put butter in a 4-cup glass measure or a deep microwave-safe bowl. Microwave butter on high 45 to 60 seconds, until melted. Whisk in sugar, then egg product until thoroughly blended.

2. Microwave on medium 1½ to 2½ minutes, stirring twice and scraping down sides of bowl with a rubber spatula, until sugar is dissolved and sauce is slightly thickened. If there are a few particles of cooked egg in sauce, strain them out.

3. Stir in rum and serve warm.

Makes 1 cup. Per 2 tablespoons: 139 calories, 1 gram protein, 13 grams carbohydrate, 9 grams fat, 23 milligrams cholesterol with butter, 0 milligrams cholesterol with margarine, 113 milligrams sodium

Index

127